MERE SPIRITUALITY

The spiritual life according to

HENRI

NOUWEN

Wil Hernandez

a. munson
01/1/18

Originally published in the United States of America in 2015
by SkyLight Paths Publishing, a division of LongHill Partners Inc., Woodstock, Vermont

First published in Great Britain in 2016

Society for Promoting Christian Knowledge
36 Causton Street
London SW1P 4ST
www.spck.org.uk

British Library Cataloguing-in-Publication Data
A catalogue record for this book is available from the British Library

ISBN 978–0–281–07687–1
eBook ISBN 978–0–281–07688–8

Printed in Great Britain by Ashford Colour Press
Subsequently digitally printed in Great Britain

eBook by Graphicraft Limited, Hong Kong

Produced on paper from sustainable forests

CenterQuest
An Ecumenical Hub for the Study and Practice
of Christian Spirituality

was birthed out of the lasting influence of Henri Nouwen
and his spirituality.

This work is especially dedicated
to my colleague and friend, my "partner in crime"
in bringing CenterQuest to life,

Lisa Myers

and to the

CenterQuest School of Spiritual Direction
Inaugural Cohort, 2015.

Contents

desire is to "will the one thing," perhaps you can find a mentor and patron saint in Henri Nouwen. He calls us beyond ourselves, even as he respects how complex and difficult that journey is. He shows us how to move toward God, even as we are still torn by our own earthly attachments.

Nouwen's writings have influenced millions and he has many admirers. Wil Hernandez is more than an admirer. He's a passionate disciple and exponent of Nouwen. For more than a dozen years he has researched, written, and taught on Nouwen's spirituality. This book is both his most synthesized and his most mature work on Nouwen. Nouwen himself wrote over sixty books, lectured widely, and inspired many books about him and his spirituality. Given the sheer volume of what he has written and what's been written about him, coupled with the fact that he didn't strive to be a systematic thinker, it can be a daunting task to attempt to pull together Nouwen's rich but scattered insights into one synthetic whole. This is what Wil Hernandez does in *Mere Spirituality*. This is a needed book, and we are grateful to Wil Hernandez for giving it to us.

Preface

Every time I conduct a retreat or a class on Henri Nouwen's spirituality—and I have done countless of them over the past ten years—I get asked by participants who are new to Nouwen's written works what to focus on in his voluminous materials and where to begin. Likewise, I run into others with some basic familiarity with Nouwen's writings—having read portions or excerpts from a number of his books—who, after getting reacquainted with Nouwen through my presentations, wish to go back to his writings or explore them further but feel somewhat at a loss as to how to get started in the process. Nouwen published more than forty books on a variety of topics in his lifetime (plus many more that have been published posthumously), and both types of participants ask questions such as "Which book should I read first?" or "What top three books on the subject of _____ would you recommend for me?" or "Which one is a good summary of his main thoughts?"

Many of these folks are looking for guidance on how they can approach Nouwen's work without feeling overwhelmed by the massive amount of material before them (including the whole array of good Nouwen compilations, anthologies, and readers currently available). It is for these people that I have written this particular book, one thematically assembled to direct readers to the corresponding primary Nouwen sources should they wish to explore further.

I also have in mind avid readers of Henri Nouwen's work who simply wish to get their hands on a single book aimed at distilling and summarizing his key insights into the spiritual life, the theme to which Nouwen devoted much of his writing energy. True, he addressed a wide range of topics, from prayer to social justice to icons to clowns, but only insofar as they bore directly on his main focal thrust: our life in the Spirit. I dare to say, in fact, that Henri Nouwen is all about spirituality, *mere* spirituality.[1]

Letting Nouwen Speak for Himself

Henri Nouwen is primarily known as a writer on the broad subject of Christian spirituality. Not one to wrangle over divisive doctrinal issues or theological disputes, Nouwen refused to be embroiled in peripheral matters that could potentially distract him from this focus. His work appeals to a broad audience—from the ultraconservative to the more progressive, from the centrist to the staunch liberal. To this day, I marvel at his ability to create space for such a diversity of views. Only someone of Henri Nouwen's caliber could have successfully convened people of various opposing camps and persuasions to sit at the same table, wrestling together with the common topic of our spiritual life—even if they could not see eye to eye on a lot of other things.

That we have far more in common with one another than we care to openly admit—despite our real differences—becomes more apparent through Nouwen's efforts at uniting us around our common spiritual longing. His work capitalizes on this intrinsic shared desire: to know and experience what it means to live out our life in God in a way that deeply transforms us inside and out.

Nouwen did not delve into the subject of our spiritual life in a strictly systematized way. He expounded creatively on various facets of it from every conceivable angle. In most of his writings, he repeated himself without apology, if only to underline his key constructs. But he did so almost always from a new perspective and context. Like Nouwen's writings, this book may seem repetitive in places, but such repetition only reflects the pervasive nature of Nouwen's spirituality. His works often yield what

---

1. I must confess that I wish I had thought of this phrase myself (it is, of course, reminiscent of one of C. S. Lewis's most popular works, *Mere Christianity*), but I credit Paul Johansen, who brought it to my attention through his essay "What a Friend We Have in Henri: Reflections on the Influence of Henri Nouwen on Protestant Evangelicals," in *Turning the Wheel: Henri Nouwen and Our Search for God*, ed. Jonathan Bengtson and Gabrielle Earnshaw (Maryknoll, NY: Orbis Books, 2007), 41.

postmodern philosophers call a surplus of meaning through each encounter with them.

While his particular treatment of spirituality can be considered multifaceted, Nouwen's major theses are hardly complex. There are clear primary themes—and my goal for this book is to present an overview of them. Yet, despite my best efforts to outline Nouwen's all-encompassing approach to our life in the Spirit in neat and tidy categories, the thematic borders seem porous.

This book is markedly different from my previous works. Drawing from my doctoral dissertation work, I wrote a trilogy on Nouwen published by Paulist Press in 2006, 2008, and 2012, in which I addressed his integrated, albeit imperfect, journey; his ministry of integration; and the spiritual polarities he embodied and held in tension. I approached my earlier works from a decidedly interpretive, academic framework, using descriptive analysis along with my own interpretation and synthesis of all the data available.

Here, however, I am not self-consciously endeavoring to interpret Henri Nouwen's writings. Instead, I am letting him freely speak for himself on the specific subject of the spiritual life and its essential features. All I am doing is arranging his choice insights and integrating them into a coherent whole. I rely solely on Nouwen's own voice, without necessarily appealing to other voices—my own included—in order to address the matter purely. Thus, this work is in no way dependent on extra materials outside of Nouwen's to guide its overall direction. Everything is based on primary sources—straight from what Henri Nouwen has either written or spoken about on the all-important topic of our spiritual life. As you might well imagine, this type of synthesis entails patiently combing through the huge amount of material Nouwen produced around the theme of our spiritual life as I attempt to structure it into a cohesive summary.

Henri Nouwen was noticeably fond of organizing his material into three main points that readers could easily remember. I adopt the same basic structure here by dividing the book into three major sections: "Communion," "Community," and "Commission." These sections correspond to Nouwen's commentary on Luke 6:12–19, in which he underscored the threefold movement from *solitude* to *community* to *ministry* as exemplified by Jesus himself. In virtually all of his writings, Nouwen addressed these themes in a much more developed way than any others. To me, the spiritual constructs of solitude, community, and ministry—which I am recasting into communion, community, and commission—sum up for us what an authentic spiritual life looks like: *a life apart* in solitude with self and communion with God; *a life shared* in community with other kindred hearts; and *a life given* for others in ministry.

I have also chosen to employ Nouwen's understanding of the "heart" as representing the full embodiment of our lived spirituality. Nouwen himself demonstrated the reality of this understanding, for his was a spirituality of the heart in its truest sense. I explore this claim in the introduction.

Part I, "Communion: A Life Apart," serves as the foundational reference for Nouwen's more expansive treatment of this theme. Here I identify three subtopics (solitude, identity, and presence) and the corresponding qualities of the heart that are necessary to live out Nouwen's heart-centered spirituality. Both parts II and III follow a similar thematic structure and format.

In keeping with my treatment of references in my trilogy of Nouwen books, I employ parenthetical citations of my primary Nouwen sources within the text itself. These are represented by the initials of the book followed by the page reference(s). For example, "*LR*:12" refers to Nouwen's book *The Living Reminder*, page 12. I have provided a complete alphabetical listing of all the cited texts with their abbreviated title initials at the end of this book for easy reference. For the specific editions I made use of, see the selected bibliography titled "Key Works of Henri J. M. Nouwen."

To the most basic question of what constitutes the essence of our spiritual life, I point to Henri Nouwen's trilogy of concepts—communion, community, commission—as the solid answer. This is spirituality pure and simple, as only Henri Nouwen could articulate it—mere spirituality indeed!

INTRODUCTION

A Heart-Filled Life

Henri Nouwen believed that the nature of our spiritual life consists of a life apart in solitude with God (communion), a life shared in community with God's people, and a life given in ministry to others (commission). What ties these themes together—what shapes the holistic picture of what the spiritual life is all about, according to Henri Nouwen—is the heart.

For Henri Nouwen, the concepts of spirituality and the heart are necessarily integrated, not just in his thinking but more so in his very being. Nouwen's references to the heart are abundant in his writings. Like the great Saint Augustine, Nouwen freely employed the term "heart" synonymously and interchangeably with the "self" and the "soul," but "heart" remained his ultimate word of choice—particularly in conjunction with our spiritual being.

In reading his works, we discover that Nouwen's "heart" is quite broad and richly nuanced. In fact, it sometimes seems like he assigns a different meaning each time he invokes the elusive language of the heart. Nouwen understands the heart in its biblical sense to be the core of our being, akin to our spiritual center, which is the most intimate place "where God speaks to us, where we hear the voice who calls us the Beloved" (B:21). He elaborates: "By heart, I do not mean the seat of our feelings as opposed to the seat of our thoughts: I mean the center of our being, that place where we are most ourselves, where we are most human, where we are most real" (*LM*:5). In his view, the heart is the operational focus of the spiritual life.

The Life of the Heart

Henri Nouwen worries that when the moral life grabs more of our attention, "we are in danger of forgetting the primacy of the mystical life, which is the life of the heart" (*RD*:48). Here Nouwen elevates the crucial importance of the mystical path and how the experience of it holds a central place in our lives.

What is this mystical life essentially about? According to Nouwen, the mystical life is what lies both at the beginning and at the end of our existence. When we enter the mystical life, we enter into an intimate and unifying communion with God, who created us in and out of love (*RD*:48). This is at once the heart of our life and the life of the heart, which Nouwen identifies as "the place where all is one in God, the place where we truly belong, the place from which we come and to which we always yearn to return" (*RD*:49). Most authentically, therefore, "living a spiritual life is living in an intimate communion with the Lord" (*SWC*:15).

It is in this place of intimacy that we enter not only into oneness with God but also into oneness with our own self, where we fully embrace who we truly are in God. Nouwen reminds us, "It's very important that the mystical life, which is the life of communion with God, is the life in which you hear a claim for yourself and your belovedness—that's what the mystical life is about" (*B*:17). Even in the case of Jesus, the Son of God, when we are told that he spent a whole night in communing prayer, it simply means: "Jesus spent the night listening to the Father calling him the Beloved" (*SL*:22). This is true oneness with the Source of our being, where the truth of our being beloved becomes our real connector and unifier.

Henri Nouwen believes that the highest summons of mystical living is to unity, and that it all begins with the heart—the "place of unification, where [we] become one." From this core of our being, "where all sentiments are held together in truth," we can "feel, think, and act truthfully" (*IVL*:14–15). Thus when we are at one with our self, it becomes effortless for us to welcome and embrace the same self where God resides, the self that God loves with the first love, preceding all human love. With Nouwen, we are able to carry our own beautiful, deeply loved self in our heart (*IVL*:29).

The Mystery of Our Heart

The spiritual life is meant to be heart-filled (or "heartful"). But herein lies the mystery of our own heart, as Nouwen illuminates:

> Our heart is the center of our being human. There our deepest thoughts, intuitions, emotions, and decisions find their source. But it's also there that we are most alienated from ourselves. We know little or nothing of our heart. We keep our distance from it, as though we were afraid of it. What is more intimate is also what frightens us most. Where we are most ourselves, we are often strangers to ourselves. That is the painful part of our being human. We fail to know our hidden center; and so we live and die often without knowing who we really are. If we ask ourselves why we think, feel, and act in a certain way, we often have no answer, thus proving to be strangers in our own house. (*LM*:74)

Nouwen laments that many of us are woefully detached from the very center of our human existence, even clueless about our own hearts most of the time. Yet it is in the very privacy and seclusion of our heart that Jesus longs to encounter us most powerfully—"to make his love known to us there, to free us from our fears, and to make our own deepest self known to us" (*LM*:74). Put simply, it is in and from our heart that we come to know both our true God and our true self when we dare to enter into its depths more trustingly.

In the same depths we are bound to discover the dynamics of what I refer to as tripolar love—love of God, love of others, love of our self—profoundly emerging from and operating within our hearts. This is the same unified love that the Bible emphasizes relentlessly as the ultimate yardstick of authentic spirituality. Nouwen describes its integrated outworking:

> Self-knowledge and self-love are the fruits of knowing and loving God.... Laying our hearts totally open to God leads to a love of ourselves that enables us to give whole-hearted love to our fellow

human beings. In the seclusion of our hearts we learn to know the hidden presence of God; and with that spiritual knowledge we can lead a loving life. (*LM*:75)

Indeed it is from this deep well within that we find the courage to live our spiritual life in accordance with the biblical law of love. After all, our heart, as Nouwen points out, is the seat of courage, and from this center of our being we are able to "listen to our heart, to speak from our heart, and to act from our heart" courageously and lovingly (*SJ*:220).

Heart to Heart

In speaking broadly about the spiritual life, Henri Nouwen admits to his natural tendency to succumb to complicated thinking. Sometimes it is difficult to stay simple, he confesses, because "simplicity asks for a pure heart and an innocent eye, qualities that are gifts from God, freely given"— we cannot will them into existence (*FSC*:42–43). The truth is, "the heart knows so much more than the mind" (*RD*:83). Nouwen often likes to appeal to the insistence of nineteenth-century Eastern Orthodox theologian Theophan the Recluse that we must always allow our mind to freely descend into our heart (*RO*:145).

In our daily lives, we often find ourselves caught up not only in complicated thinking but also in confusing, ambivalent feelings raging within us. If we do not learn how to sort them out carefully, unbridled emotions can potentially have paralyzing effects on our spiritual life. Identifying where such feelings originate can help loosen their hold over us. But Nouwen is quick to point out that "this identification is not an intellectual task; it is a task of the heart," and we must engage in it with all our heart and devoid of all fear (*IVL*:36).

Nouwen believes that "our journey to become more fully human is a spiritual journey that begins and ends in the heart of God" (*SL*:vii). As he testifies, "Whatever is pure, simple, and innocent in me comes from him. With his love I can love and give myself to others. With his eyes I can see God's face; with his ears I can hear God's voice; with his heart I can speak to God's heart" (*FSC*:45).

To Nouwen, nowhere is this reality experienced more profoundly— and mystically—than in the celebration of the Eucharist, which represents the spiritual center of gravity in his own life. The Eucharist has ramifications for our outward life as well. Nouwen explains:

> When your heart is touched by the presence of Jesus in the Eucharist, then you will receive new eyes capable of recognizing that same presence in the hearts of others. Heart speaks to heart. Jesus in our heart speaks to Jesus in the hearts of our fellow men and women. That's the eucharistic mystery of which we are a part. (LM:77)

In his book *With Burning Hearts: A Meditation on the Eucharistic Life*, Nouwen draws on the famous Emmaus Road episode recorded in Luke's Gospel to highlight the five aspects of the eucharistic celebration: loss, presence, invitation, communion, and mission. As the story goes in Luke 24, two disciples of Jesus are walking from Jerusalem to Emmaus on the day that Jesus rose from the dead. They are joined by the resurrected Jesus, although they do not recognize him. The not-yet-identified Jesus asks the sad-looking disciples, "What are you discussing with each other while you walk along?" (Luke 24:17). They tell the stranger of Jesus's crucifixion and the report of his empty tomb. Jesus proceeds to give them a lesson on the prophecies of the Christian scriptures that are fulfilled in his death and resurrection. Later, over dinner, after Jesus breaks the bread and blesses the meal, they realize who the stranger actually is, and Jesus vanishes.

Nouwen identifies a movement that frames the entire story as one from resentment to gratitude, that is, "from a hardened heart to a grateful heart" (BH:13). Eucharist, according to Nouwen, is also about recognition—the total realization that communion is "the deepest cry of God's and our heart, because we are made with a heart that can be satisfied only by the One who made it" (BH:71).

Seeking the Heart of the Kingdom

"Spirituality is attention to the life of the spirit in us," Nouwen declares (LR:12). Where do we attend to this life? In our heart, of course. Nouwen elevates the privileged place of the heart as the practical outworking of our life with God. Not only that, he directs us all to what he believes is the true way of the heart, which is also the way of the Spirit. Nouwen is convinced that "living a spiritual life requires a change of heart, a conversion"

(*MTN*:57), one that is wrought only from the inside out by God's own Spirit. Nothing less is guaranteed to work.

This is why Jesus "asks us to move our hearts to the center, where all other things fall into place" (*MTN*:42–43). What is this center? Jesus calls it the kingdom. According to Nouwen, "A heart set on the Father's kingdom is also a heart set on the spiritual life. To set our hearts on the kingdom therefore means to make the life of the Spirit within and among us the center of all we think, say, or do" (*MTN*:43). Without Jesus at the helm, reigning in our heart, such kingdom life is impossible. In fact, for Nouwen, "living with Jesus at the center" is what it means to truly live spiritually (*LM*:7)—that is, within the realm of the Spirit. Expressed in another way, "spiritual life is life lived in the spirit of Jesus" (*LM*:82). True spirituality, Nouwen concludes, is simultaneously a matter of the Spirit and of the heart. A heart-focused life is likewise a Spirit-oriented life.

The Heart of Discipline

In *The Way of the Heart*, Henri Nouwen presents three ways to life in the Spirit: flee, be silent, pray (*WOH*:15). These are based on the ancient teachings of Saint Anthony and the desert fathers and mothers. In practice, Nouwen views all three as integrated and foundational habits of the heart that represent a unified pathway to a heart-centered spiritual life. Solitude, silence, and prayer, taken together as a spiritual package, are, for Nouwen, what essentially constitute the solid foundation of our spiritual life in God.

The way of the heart identified by Henri Nouwen is what undergirds the core spiritual disciplines that make our life in the Spirit work as a whole. One of the basic tensions we confront is in our realization that our spiritual life is indeed a gift but that it also requires human effort on our part (*MTN*:65). As Nouwen puts it, "A spiritual life without discipline is impossible" (*MTN*:66). More pointedly, "the spiritual life demands a discipline of the heart" to assist us "to let God into our hearts and become known to us there, in the deepest recesses of our own being" (*LM*:75).

By spiritual discipline, we are referring to what Nouwen describes as "the concentrated effort to create some inner and outer space in our lives" where obedience can be practiced (*MTN*:68). Nouwen identifies three spiritual disciplines by which we create space for God, beginning with spending time with God in solitude; then creating a fellowship with people with whom we are sharing the mission; and finally going out together, healing and proclaiming the Good News (*SL*:18).

This paradigmatic movement emerges out of a passage in the Gospel of Luke (Luke 6:12–19) in which Nouwen assigns the symbolic sequence of first praying in solitude at *night*, forming a newfound community in the *morning*, and engaging in the work of ministry in the *afternoon* (or the rest of the day):

> Jesus went out to a mountainside to pray, and spent the *night* praying to God. When *morning* came, he called his disciples to him and chose twelve of them, whom he also designated apostles.... He went down with them and stood on a level place. A large crowd of his disciples was there and a great number of people from all over ... who had come to hear him and to be healed of their diseases. Those troubled by evil spirits were cured, and the people all tried to touch him, because power was coming from him and healing them all. (Luke 6:12–19 NIV, quoted in *SD*:110; Nouwen's emphasis added)

Nouwen summarizes, "Communion with God alone in prayer leads inevitably to community with God's people, and then to ministry in the world" (*D*:10). While we can note the progression in its process of unfolding, the spiritual life is not to be construed as strictly linear or even simply reciprocal but rather cyclical in its dynamic outworking. Communion, community, and commission—this trilogy paints a well-integrated picture of the essentials of our spiritual life.

By Way of the Heart

An Overview of
Henri Nouwen's Life

Henri Nouwen, world-renowned Dutch priest, is considered to be one of the greatest spiritual writers of the last century. Second only in popularity to the famed Trappist monk Thomas Merton, Nouwen succeeded in making spirituality accessible to the masses. During his lifetime, he wrote over forty books, which have sold over two million copies and been translated into more than twenty-two languages. All of his writings, though varied in both treatment and style, focused on the subject of our spiritual life.

Born January 24, 1932, to a devout Catholic family in Nijkerk, southeast of Amsterdam in the Netherlands, Henri Josef Machiel responded to a call to the priesthood at a young age and was ordained in 1957 as a diocesan priest in the Archdiocese of Utrecht. Even as a young child, he was drawn to the Eucharist, and this became his spiritual center of gravity throughout his life, so much so that as a priest there was hardly a day when he did not celebrate the Eucharist alone or with friends.

In his ardent desire to more deeply understand himself and the people he was seeking to minister to, Nouwen made an unusual request of his bishop: to pursue graduate studies in psychology—a field that, at the time, was not a popular arena of concentrated study, especially among Catholics. Much to his pleasant surprise, his desire was granted, and for the next seven years he went on to study psychology at the University of Nijmegen. Not content in the confines of the university, Nouwen again boldly asked his bishop, on the suggestion of well-known Harvard psychologist Gordon Allport, if he could apply for a fellowship at the Menninger Foundation in Topeka, Kansas. Again with the bishop's blessing, he moved to the United States in 1964 for a two-year fellowship to study religion and psychiatry at the Menninger Clinic, the birthplace of clinical pastoral education (CPE). The founder of CPE, Anton Boisen, had a profound influence on Nouwen's eventual way of doing ministry. An immensely complex person who popularized the concept of the "theology of living human documents" (meaning that we do theology directly out of lived experience), Boisen was also responsible for introducing the case study method in CPE, which bolstered Nouwen's early leanings toward a more phenomenological—as opposed to clinical, quantitative, or empirical—approach to psychology. Evidence of Boisen's impact on Nouwen can be found in a number of his books, most notably in the hugely popular *The Wounded Healer*, which came to be a cornerstone of Nouwen's spirituality.

Henri Nouwen's entrance to America through the Menninger Clinic was in every way perfectly timed. Not only were the people there engaged in spirited conversations on the intersection between theology and psychology, but they were also quite accustomed to viewing life through psychological lenses and poised to embrace the burgeoning interest in the field of spirituality. Americans were eager to receive Nouwen and what he had to offer to a new generation of seekers.

After Nouwen's two-year residency at the Menninger Clinic, the director of research programs moved to the University of Notre Dame to establish a department of psychology graduate program and invited Nouwen to join him. For the next two years, Nouwen devoted much of his time not just to teaching pastoral theology and psychology at Notre Dame but also to public lecturing and writing. It was during his last semester at Notre Dame that he learned about the assassination of Martin Luther King Jr. This led him to fly to Atlanta to join the throngs of people who participated in the historic funeral march from Selma to Montgomery in solidarity with the civil rights protesters.

As Nouwen was slowly being immersed into the social and political climate of America, the need to complete his doctorate compelled him to return to the Netherlands in 1968. He ended up teaching pastoral psychology and spirituality there as well, first at the Amsterdam Joint Pastoral Institute and then at the Catholic Theological Institute in Utrecht, where he became the chair of the department of behavioral sciences. A year after his return, he published his first book, *Intimacy: Essays in Pastoral Psychology*, a compendium of his many lectures and sermons given while he was a visiting professor at Notre Dame.

During this time, Nouwen's popularity as a writer grew widely throughout the United States, where *Intimacy* was well-received. The dean of Yale Divinity School extended several invitations to Nouwen to teach pastoral theology there, and Nouwen finally accepted and moved back to America in 1971. Yale became his parish, and he welcomed both Protestants and Catholics to share in his daily celebration of the Eucharist in the chapel basement. His decadelong stay at Yale was a highly productive period, not just as a popular professor but as a prolific writer of more than a dozen books.

For seven months in 1974, coinciding with the year he received tenure at Yale, Nouwen spent his sabbatical living and working with the Trappist monks in the Abbey of the Genesee in upstate New York to escape his frenzied lifestyle. Out of his daily journaling and spiritual direction sessions with the abbot, John Eudes Bamberger, came *The Genesee Diary*, which was published two years after the sabbatical and was an instant best seller, catapulting Nouwen into greater fame as a writer and speaker. After the sudden death of his mother in 1978, Nouwen went back to the abbey to spend another six months reflecting on his spiritual life even more deeply and writing daily prayers, which became another devotional book, *A Cry for Mercy*, published in 1981.

In that same year, to the surprise of many, Nouwen gave up his tenure at Yale to explore missionary prospects in Latin America. This was part of his growing burden to identify with the poor and the marginalized and to follow more seriously the "downward mobility" exemplified by Jesus. After a year of traveling, during which he chronicled his experience of living with the poor of Bolivia and Peru, Nouwen discerned that he was not cut out for full-time missionary work in that part of the world. Instead, on returning to the United States, he went on a "reverse mission," conveying to the North on behalf of the South his firsthand experience of the oppressive political and economic situation in Latin America.

In 1982 Harvard started wooing Nouwen, and he eventually accepted their offer on the condition that he would teach for only one semester a year so he could devote the rest of his time to activism and writing. Nouwen was popular among the students at Harvard, but not the faculty, who viewed his passion for speaking boldly and openly about Jesus as politically incorrect. At Harvard people talked about God in abstraction and not in the personal way that Nouwen did. Added to this, Nouwen was not deemed intellectual enough as a professor. This unwelcoming attitude affected Nouwen deeply. At the invitation of Jean Vanier, the founder of the L'Arche International community, Nouwen left Harvard to spend a year at Trosly, France, to discern whether God might in fact be calling him to serve among people with developmental disabilities. That was where he met Nathan Ball, who became one of his dearest friends and the person with whom he would work closely at the L'Arche Daybreak community in Toronto for the last decade of his life.

Henri Nouwen did settle down in 1986 at L'Arche Daybreak in answer to the call of the community for him to become their resident priest. Nathan Ball took on the role of community leader at Daybreak. Nouwen also became close with Sue Mosteller, a sister of Saint Joseph, who co-pastored the community with Nouwen. Fourteen months into his time at L'Arche Daybreak, Nouwen suffered a nervous breakdown after the collapse of his tight friendship with Ball. This resulted in him being pulled out of the community temporarily to be under the care of a two-person team—a psychotherapist and a spiritual director—in a treatment facility in Winnipeg for about seven months. Nouwen recovered and returned to the community a much stronger person, and his relationship with Ball eventually healed. This dark but triumphant episode of his life became the focus of *The Inner Voice of Love*, which Nouwen finally allowed to be published eight years after the events took place.

When he was a year short of a decade at Daybreak, the community sent Nouwen off to spend a sabbatical year to do more focused writing. On his way to the Hermitage Museum in Saint Petersburg, where he had planned to film a documentary inspired by his popular book *The Return of the Prodigal Son*, based on the equally famous painting of Rembrandt, Nouwen suffered a heart attack on a layover in his home country. On September 21, 1996, Nouwen had another heart attack, this time fatal. His body was flown to Toronto five days later. Following a few days of mourning at Daybreak, Nouwen was buried in the little Sacred Heart Cemetery near Toronto. The cemetery was flocked to by thousands of mourners from all over the globe whose lives had been blessed by Nouwen's life and ministry.

Henri Nouwen's greatest contribution to the field of Christian spirituality is the shining example of his own life. His was a multifaceted spirituality characterized by various shades of personal embodiment: a spirituality of the heart, prayer, waiting, compassionate caregiving, integration, powerlessness, peacemaking, healing and reconciliation, social justice, ministry, hospitality, imperfection. This was all an outgrowth of his strong but uncomplicated faith—his mere spirituality.

Part I

Communion

A Life Apart

"Our hunger for communion is a precious gift from God and a true driving force of our spiritual journey."
—*A Spirituality of Living*

"Somewhere we know that without a lonely place our lives are in danger. Somewhere we know that without silence words lose their meaning, that without listening speaking no longer heals, that without distance closeness cannot cure. Somewhere we know that without a lonely place our actions quickly become empty gestures."
—*Out of Solitude*

"You have to close yourself to the outside world so you can enter your own heart and the heart of God."
—*The Inner Voice of Love*

"Jesus went out to the mountainside to pray,
and spent the night praying to God."

—Luke 6:12 NIV

While he was on earth, Jesus modeled for us the necessity of having quality time set apart for God. We are told in the Gospel of Luke that he devoted a whole night praying to God. It's difficult to imagine Jesus petitioning his Father all night long, although that understandably might have taken up part of the time he spent in prayer. Henri Nouwen believes that during this time Jesus simply communed with his Father and enjoyed God's presence. Jesus knew that communion with God was essential for his being, in the same way that we are all created to be in union with our Creator.

Every human heart longs to belong, to feel connected, to experience safety and a sense of at-homeness. None of these desires can be fulfilled on our own. "Our whole being yearns for another mind; our heart needs another heart" (*SL*:21). The word that best describes this intrinsic hunger inside of us is "communion," which means "union with." In Nouwen's words, which are reminiscent of the oft-quoted statement of Saint Augustine, "God has given us a heart that will remain restless until it has found full communion" (*HN*:43).

Nouwen reminds us that this built-in longing for communion has been part of us since we were born. It originates from God and is an extension of our true vocation, our most authentic desire (*IVL*:95). Indeed, "our final journey home becomes an 'exodus' in which 'we leave this world for full communion with God'" (*FWH*:12).

Communion involves a mutuality of desire between the human and the Divine. "[It] is what God wants and what we want.... God created in our heart a yearning for communion that no one but God can, and wants, to fulfill" (*BH*:70–71). We are made for this kind of cooperative union that is meant to be experienced in mutually satisfying ways.

3

Nouwen was once asked how he envisioned living his life in the next decade. His swift answer was, "In deep communion with Jesus. Jesus has to be and to become evermore the center of my life" (FSC:7). Nouwen understood that "communion with Jesus means becoming like him" and it "leads to a new realm of being ... [and] ushers us into the Kingdom" (BH:74). Communion transforms us through and through.

"[The] discipline of daily, faithful communion with the Beloved is the foundation of the spiritual life underneath all we do, say, and create" (CR:104). In it is expressed the mystery of God's total self-giving love (BH:68). The famous parable of the prodigal son gives us a compelling glimpse of how God patiently longs to be in communion with us, forever waiting for us. The most consoling truth is that "even when we leave home for a while, Love waits for our return" (HT:120). It is amazing love indeed!

Communion and Prayer

There is no way we can talk about communion without addressing the all-encompassing experience of prayer. For Henri Nouwen, prayer represents the true essence of being one with God. Communion is all about being in "union with God in prayer," which, interestingly, is how the word "theology" is similarly defined by early church fathers like Evagrius of Pontus in its most original, classic sense (INJ:30). For at the heart of true theology lies the experience of communion and prayer. The interchangeable liturgical expressions like "communing prayer" and "prayer of communion" only serve to highlight Nouwen's basic belief that to pray is to commune with God and true communion with God involves praying.

> "God desires communion: a unity that is vital and alive, an intimacy that comes from both sides, a bond that is truly mutual ... a communion freely offered and received."
>
> —*With Burning Hearts*

Prayer is considered by Nouwen to be the "breath of human existence" (WH:17) and consequently occupies the very center of our spiritual life (RO:115). It is what Jesus refers to as "the only necessary thing" (Luke 10:42). "It is living with God, here and now" (PW:33). For "it is only in and through prayer that we can become intimately connected with Jesus and find the strength to join him on his way" (RD:89). Nouwen is convinced that when it comes to our spiritual health and well-being, "a life lived in connection with Christ should be our first and overriding concern" (*LR*:34).

Prayer summons us to an ever-deepening communion with the One who loves us more than anyone else can (*RD*:120). In essence, communing prayer is all about an intimate relationship with the God of love, "who molded our being in our mother's womb with love and only love. There, in the first love, lies our true self, a self ... solidly rooted in the One who called us into existence" (*RP*:17). What a privileged connection we have with the very source of our being—to think that such connectedness is securely bonded in eternal love! As Nouwen gratefully acknowledges, "In prayer I can enter into contact with the God who created me and all things out of love. In prayer I can find a new sense of belonging since it is there that I am most related" (*GD*:130).

> "Indeed, God wants to be admitted into the human heart, received with open hands, and loved with the same love with which we have been created."
>
> —*With Open Hands*

The prayer of communion relates to our inner experience of being at home in and with God. As Nouwen further clarifies, "Prayer is seeking our home where the Lord has built a home—in the intimacy of our own hearts." As such, prayer becomes for us "the most concrete way to make our home in God." There we are launched on an interior journey to our heart, "that intimate home where an unceasing conversation of love can take place.... This intimate bond with God, constantly nurtured by prayer, offers us a true home" (*LS*:39–41). In God's house, which is the house of love, all of us were created. To that same house we are summoned to return. "Prayer is the act of returning" (*RP*:17). Thus it can be said that communion is about our own homecoming.

A life of ongoing communion requires great intentionality on our part. The experience itself does not just happen. We have to set aside time and space for communion. It is "a life apart" involving the intimacy of

> "Prayer is the way to let the life-giving Spirit of God penetrate all the corners of my being. Prayer is the divine instrument of my wholeness, unity, and inner peace."
>
> —*Sabbatical Journey*

solitude, the centeredness and groundedness of our own identity in God as "Beloveds" of God, and the posture of loving attentiveness within the experiential context of true presence.

Personal Ponderings

1. How do I personally experience communing with God, in accordance with my own personality, my particular bents, and my unique wiring and temperament—where I can truly feel God's pleasure and delight? Can I pinpoint my holy pathway to God that emerges out of God's special design and calling for me? Have I discovered my own natural prayer language?

2. When was the last time I "wasted time" hanging out with God, without any agenda in mind except to enjoy God's presence? What was that like, and how did that make me feel? What prevents me from engaging in this experience more often?

3. What specific contemplative prayer practices resonate deeply with me and why? What makes prayer life-giving for me? How does prayer deepen my own experience of union with God? Which prayer exercises pose a continuing challenge for me to engage in and why?

ONE

Solitude

An Intimate Heart

"Solitude is the gentle guide to
all forms of intimacy."
—*Clowning in Rome*

Henri Nouwen espouses that communing with God is savored best, though by no means exclusively, within the context of solitude. In solitude, our experiential union with God comes alive. Nouwen asserts that "the measure of [our] solitude is the measure of [our] capacity for communion" (*GD*:46). The more we allow room for solitude in our hectic lives, the more our sense of connectedness with God deepens. He articulately expresses the needful place of solitude in our lives:

> In the center of breathless activities we hear a restful breathing. Surrounded by hours of moving we find a moment of quiet stillness. In the heart of much involvement there are words of withdrawal. In the midst of action there is contemplation. And after much togetherness there is solitude. (*OS*:13)

Nouwen claims that "without solitude it is virtually impossible to live a spiritual life" (*MTN*:69). That is because the practice of solitude centers us in our own hearts and enables us to be "securely rooted in personal intimacy with the source of life" (*INJ*:32). Nouwen not only knew the secret of solitude but also practiced it. He anchored himself in the discipline. The beginning point of Nouwen's spiritual seeking was always his own heart; as he reminded himself, "My lonely self ... should be my first source of search and research" (RO:29). There within its hidden corners, he listened to Jesus's invitation, "Come and let your heart find rest in mine and trust that all will be well," and willingly responded, "I want to come, Jesus, and be with you. Here I am, Lord, take my heart and let it become a heart filled with your love" (HSH:57).

As we endeavor to withdraw from our daily occupations, we are deliberately creating space for God as well as for ourselves. Such grounding times in solitude are what undergird and sustain our spiritual life with God.

Solitude and Silence

"Solitude and silence are the context within which prayer is practiced" (WOH:69). Solitude invites silence. For Nouwen, true silence has to do with the notion of rest—"rest of body and mind, in which we become available for him whose heart is greater than ours" (I:137). Silence is the way to make solitude a reality, in that it completes and intensifies the whole experience (WOH:43). Silence is, as Nouwen underlines it, "solitude practiced in action ... an indispensable discipline in the spiritual life" (WOH:44).

"Silence is the royal road to spiritual formation."

—*Spiritual Direction*

According to Nouwen, there are real consequences when we fail to observe the critical discipline of silence:

> Without silence the Spirit will die in us and the creative energy of our life will float away and leave us alone, cold, and tired. Without silence we will lose our center and become the victim of the many who constantly demand our attention. (I:138)

There is something life-giving when silence is deliberately factored into our daily experience. It provides a much-needed space for us to function in a spiritually healthy way—for our own benefit and for others' as well. Silence in God's presence belongs to the core of every prayer, Nouwen emphasizes, for "the silent time makes us quiet and deepens our awareness of ourselves and God" (RO:136). The gift that silence brings comes with a promise of new birth even as we are ushered back to the One leading us. "In this silence," Nouwen says, "you lose the feeling of being driven and you find that you can be yourself along with other people" (*OH*:43).

Solitude and Prayer

Henri Nouwen believes that "the first sign of prayer, the first indication that the presence of God's Spirit no longer remains unnoticed" often shows itself in one's increasing yearning for solitude (*MTN*:74). Its practice, he is convinced, "is one of the most powerful disciplines in developing a prayerful life" (*MTN*:75). Nouwen describes the direct relationship between solitude and prayer:

> I am called to enter into the inner sanctuary of my own being where God has chosen to dwell. The only way to that place is prayer, unceasing prayer. Many struggles and much pain can clear the way, but I am certain that only unceasing prayer can let me enter it. (*RPS*:18)

There, in that place of solitude, that "simple, uncluttered place ... we dwell in the presence of the Lord" through prayer (*MTN*:76). Nouwen emphasizes the fact that "prayer ... in the sense of a prayerful life, a life lived in connection with Christ, should be our first and overriding concern" (*LR*:34).

To Nouwen, prayer represents the breath of our life, permeating all aspect of our lives. "It is the unceasing recognition that God is wherever we are, always inviting us to come closer and to celebrate the divine gift of being alive" (*OH*:122). In short, "all indeed is prayer" (*LFL*:103).

Lest we mistake Nouwen's version of solitude and prayer as highly private, we clearly see in his use of this metaphor how they necessarily include community—even the larger community of the world. Thus, "prayer is first of all entering into communion with God, and God's people" (*B*:25). Through living in this kind of unceasing

> "When you pray, you open yourself to the influence of Power which has revealed itself as Love.... Once touched by this Power ... you have found a center for your life."
>
> —*With Open Hands*

communion, we are enabled to see and proclaim "the rightful order of things, the divine order" and live in the very heart of God—"a heart of justice, peace, and righteousness" (*LFL*:102). "Prayer is the way to both the heart of God and the heart of the world—precisely because they have been joined through the suffering of Jesus Christ"; thus to pray is to allow our own heart to become "the place where the tears of God and the tears of God's children can merge and become tears of hope" (*LFL*:100).

A Place of Intimacy

Through solitude, silence, and prayer, intimacy becomes the heart of our time apart. According to Nouwen, solitude is "the place of intimate encounter, the place where we commune with God" (*CR*:30). Akin to entering a most private sanctuary that calls forth our inmost desires, in such encounter with solitude "our deep longings to be loved unconditionally, and to love with our whole beings are uncovered, and in solitude we more readily meet the One who calls us Beloved" (*CR*:xiv).

Little wonder that Nouwen likens solitude to "the garden for our hearts, which yearn for love ... the place where our aloneness can bear fruit" (*BJ*:Jan 21). We all experience loneliness; there is a sense in which to be human is to be lonely and alone. The question is, how are we to handle the reality of our lonely existence? The simple answer is through the discipline of solitude. It is a habit you acquire over time so "you [can] deal with your loneliness in such a way that it doesn't destroy you or others, but instead becomes a place to discover the truth of who you are" (*B*:8–9).

Nouwen offers some reasons why the consistent practice of solitude is essential for our own well-being:

> Solitude is the way to embrace, to befriend your aloneness as a positive gift.... If you embrace it and enter deeply into your loneliness it can be converted to solitude. It can be converted to an aloneness that becomes a source of life. (*B*:7)

How does such conversion happen? Nouwen identifies the first step as mustering the courage to enter into our aloneness and face it instead of denying that it exists. Nouwen urges us, "Do not run, but be quiet and silent. Listen attentively to your own struggle. The answer to your question is hidden in your own heart" (*RO*:34–35). Applying the wisdom of this admonition may pave the way for the beginnings of a quiet solitude amid our gnawing sense of loneliness.

What are we expected to do when we engage ourselves in solitude? Nothing, except to be fully present to the God who is ever present to each of us and who desires our undivided attention. For "it is precisely in this 'useless' presence to God that we can ... give ear to the voice of love hidden in the center of our being" (*PW*:45). What is more, in solitude we are afforded a lingering sense of intimacy that goes beyond ourselves and extends to others around us. There is something to be said for being alone, which "indirectly transforms relationships and builds community" (*CR*:xiv). In fact, Nouwen regards solitude as "the very ground from which community grows" where "our intimacy with each other is deepened" (*CR*:12–13). Moreover, "in solitude we become aware that we were together before we came together and that life is not a creation of our will but rather an obedient response to the reality of our being united" (*CR*:14).

> "Solitude ... puts us in touch with a unity that precedes all unifying activities."
>
> —*Clowning in Rome*

We see here the necessary and inevitable correlation between solitude and community. In part II, I aim to tackle solitude's vital link to community life in more expansive detail. Suffice it to mention for now that intimacy is a key dynamic in a life deliberately set apart for God, a secret life unexposed to others. Intimacy with God is experienced most deeply within the context of hiddenness. What takes place in our private life determines the outcome of our life in public, thus the absolute need for us to maintain what Nouwen calls a hidden life, detached from the competing distractions of life.

A Hidden Life

To be able to live a robust spiritual life in the world, Nouwen declares, "I must have my own privacy where I can hide from the face of the challenging world" (*I*:118) Just what characterizes the privacy that Nouwen deems so essential? This is "a place where nobody can enter, where I am completely by myself, where I develop my own most inner privacy. This is the place where I can meet God" (*I*:118).

No less than Jesus himself modeled this for us, as evidenced in the Gospels. Amid his active engagement in ministry, "Jesus continued to return to hidden places to be alone with God" (*BJ*:Aug 13). Never did he apologize for withdrawing—abruptly at times—from the crowd. He knew that his ministry to people depended on his determination to protect his private time with his Father.

Nouwen insists that "if we don't have a hidden life with God, our public life for God cannot bear fruit" (*BJ*:Aug 13). Moreover, he elevates the necessity of hiding from the world as a crucial condition for the formation of any community. "A [person] who does not have privacy," according to Nouwen, "cannot be a part of a community" (*I*:118). There

> "To live a Christian life means to live in the world without being of it. It is in solitude that this inner freedom can grow."
>
> —*Out of Solitude*

is a sense in which we must learn to remove ourselves from the world in order to more freely and effectively be of service to the needs of the world. Thomas Merton's life embodied this paradoxical reality—his detachment from the world actually brought him closer to it.

Nouwen regarded Merton as his spiritual and literary mentor. The two met only once, briefly, at the Abbey of Our Lady of Gethsemani in Kentucky, yet through his immersion in Merton's writings, Nouwen was able to fully capture the central force of Merton's existence related to his vision of God, humanity, and the world (*EM*:13). Nouwen said of Merton, "The more he was able to convert his restless loneliness into a solitude of heart, the more he could discover the pains of his world in his own inner center and respond to them" (*RO*:59).

A Place of Conversion

Through solitude we can guard and sustain our hidden life with God. Consistently engaging in the discipline of being alone in God's presence ushers us to the place of purification and paves the way for our ongoing experience of conversion (*BJ*:Aug 15).

Henri Nouwen reckons solitude as the furnace in which transformation occurs (*WOH*:20). It represents both "the place of the great struggle and the great encounter" (*WOH*:31–32). Naturally, this creates a tension within us—something Nouwen regularly wrestled with out of his own brokenness and woundedness, with which many of us can connect. Nouwen confessed one time that much to his own dismay, "my own restlessness ... [has] made me flee solitude as soon as I have found it" (*GG*:1). He could thus testify:

> Solitude is not immediately satisfying, because in solitude we meet our demons, our addictions, our feelings of lust and anger, and our immense need for recognition and approval. But if we do not run away, we will meet there also the One who says, "Do not be afraid. I am with you, and I will guide you through the valley of darkness." (*BJ*:Jan 21)

Solitude has a way of simultaneously exposing us to both the dark and light facets of our inner life. The struggle, in Nouwen's view, has to do with the compulsions of our many false selves, while "the great encounter" involves a loving confrontation with our true God, side by side with our true self (see *WOH*:26).

Many of us find it difficult to venture into, let alone sustain, an ongoing practice of solitude. Nouwen clarifies why this is so:

> It is hard precisely because by facing God alone we are also facing our own inner chaos. We come in direct confrontation with our restlessness, anxieties, resentments, unresolved tensions, hidden animosities, and long-standing frustrations. Our spontaneous reaction to all this is to run away and get busy again, so that we can at least make ourselves believe that things are not as bad as they seem in our solitude. The truth is that things are bad, even worse than they seem. It is this painful stripping away of the old self, this falling away from all our old support systems that enables us to cry out for the unconditional mercy of God. (*SWC*:87)

> "In the solitude of our heart we can listen to our questions ... and gradually grow, without even noticing it, into the answer."
>
> —*The Selfless Way of Christ*

Yet the positive prospects for us are just as real. For if "we do not run away in fear, but patiently stay with our struggles, the outer space of solitude gradually becomes an inner space, a space in our heart where we come to know the presence of the Spirit who has already been given to us" (*SWC*:87). The ugly manifestations of the flesh can indeed be glaring, but so is the reality—and the certainty—of the Spirit's inner work.

Doubtless, there is a tension fueled by our constant wrestling with the coexistence of our true self and our false self in the thick of solitude. However, there is some good news for us to appreciate. As Nouwen points out, such tension can become the very dynamic that leads to our renewal and conversion. Thus we can rightly view it as transformative tension, and solitude happens to be its venue.

Encountering God Plus Our Self

Solitude is primarily about setting aside time to be alone with God, to feel God's very presence. Nouwen is quick to state, "Our first task in solitude is to simply allow ourselves to become aware of the divine presence, to 'Be still, and know that I am God'" (*D*:10). For the Christian, solitude is not just about visiting a wilderness spot or being on a mountaintop to be privately disengaged from everything else. More than anything it has to do with "daring to stand in God's presence. Not to guard time simply to be alone, but alone in God's company" (*TMD*:76).

At the same time, solitude certainly involves more than that. For through solitude we come face-to-face not only with God but with our true self as well. In fact, it is precisely in the light of God's presence that we can see ourselves for who we really are. That said, solitude encompasses a kind of double transformative encounter: with ourselves and with God—often even simultaneously.

> "In solitude, we not only encounter God but come to know ourselves in our truth."
>
> —*Clowning in Rome*

Every conversion, from our vantage point, starts with seeing, with our capacity to view ourselves the way God views us. Entailed in this is our resolve to squarely face our core identity in God. Solitude is decidedly that context in which we come to realize our true self. "It is the place where we take a few moments in quiet before God to see who we are in relationship to God and to each other" (*CR*:19). The focus is on our inner being. Often in life we get preoccupied with doing and having while conveniently neglecting the primacy of our being. Henri Nouwen calls attention to the fact that the place of solitude is where "we discover that being is more important than having, that we are worth more than the result of our efforts .... that our worth is not the same as our usefulness" (OS:22). In God's eyes, we are eternally loved whether we are productive or not. Never is performance the measure of our value and acceptance before God. From the world's perspective, of course, performance is what counts—and we can easily succumb to that belief. Nouwen advises, "When we enter into solitude we will often hear these two voices—the voice of the world and the voice of the Lord—pulling us in two contrary directions. But if we keep returning faithfully to the place of solitude, the voice of the Lord will gradually become stronger" (PW:45).

Henri Nouwen admonishes those of us whose identities are hidden in God to learn what it means to courageously enter into the place of solitude empty-handed, with our inner spaces devoid of overoccupation (SWC:85; cf. RO:73ff.). We would do well to consciously open up space in our hearts, making ourselves ready to receive whatever it is God may pour in. Most importantly, it becomes imperative that we develop a heart transparent enough to be able to see God and ourselves through the same lens.

> "Solitude is the place where we go in order to hear the truth about ourselves."
>
> —Beloved

Solitude of the Heart

Far from what most imagine solitude to be in its idealized sense—that of actual, literal withdrawal from the world—solitude is in every way a practical reality that anybody can enter into, even within our mundane existence. Henri Nouwen hastens to enlighten us, if only to expand our often myopic categories: "The solitude that really counts is the solitude of the heart; it is an inner quality or attitude that does not depend on physical isolation" (RO:37).

The practice of solitude is not the monopoly of hermits stationed in the desert. What Nouwen is stressing here is the imperative for us, wherever we may find ourselves, to cultivate a disposition of inner groundedness that helps us function in our everyday life from a peaceful center in our heart space despite the chaos of our external world (see RO:38).

For Further Focused Reading

Clowning in Rome: Reflections on Solitude, Celibacy, Prayer, and Contemplation

Out of Solitude: Three Meditations on the Christian Life

The Way of the Heart: Desert Spirituality and Contemporary Ministry

Living It Out

1. Put a day on your calendar to literally get away from the competing demands of your life. Choose a place that is some distance from your familiar surroundings, where you can be by yourself. Drop any agenda from your mind and just decide to hang out with God for a day. Simply enjoy the time "wasted with God" and journal about it.

2. Without actually scheduling it, try to practice what Nouwen calls "solitude of the heart" in whatever way seems right for you. Be aware of God's presence in whatever you are doing, allowing yourself to experience fully the reality of God inside and around you.

3. Do a brief "examen," a conscious review of a particular day, focusing on one experience where you felt genuinely intimate with God. Engage your thoughts, emotions, and feelings, and describe what intimacy with God looks like and means to you personally. Record your reflections in your journal as you savor the memory of communing with God.

Prayer of the Heart

Abiding God,

The invitation to be with you is overwhelming yet resonates with my deepest and truest desires. I often don't pay enough attention to just how much I want to be with you. At the same time, I also resist going into solitude. I don't know what is there for us to do together. I am scared that I might find you to be boring or inaccessible. I am worried that the web of entanglements in which I live might unravel if I go away to be alone. I have parts of me that I like to hide—even from myself—and I am fearful that they might come to the surface if I am alone and quiet for long.

But you keep inviting me nonetheless. All of those fears eventually lose their energy as I sit in the quietness of your love. Your presence and your silence gently invite me to find my home in you and to discover that you are already dwelling in me. Here I find you, I find others, I find the world in which I live, and I find my own life hidden in yours.

Abide in me, O God, and help me to abide in you.

Amen.

TWO

Identity

A Centered Heart

"Like Jesus, I am a beloved son of
God.... A contained life is returning
to and living this primal truth."
—*Home Tonight*

Our self-identity is what grounds us as unique individuals. Our human identity is inherently spiritual by virtue of the *imago Dei* (image of God) woven into our very being. We are God's image-bearers, however imperfectly we reflect this image. And Henri Nouwen reminds us that our entire life ought to be anchored in our spiritual identity (see *SD*:34), for that is what establishes in us a strong sense of self, of being in this world. Without this kind of rootedness, it is hard, if not impossible, to sustain our spiritual life.

To live spiritually means to live out of who we genuinely are. As simple as it may sound, all of us stumble over this fundamental issue. Not only does our real identity get blurred at times, but we also become misled, often subtly, by the distorted notions we have accumulated over time concerning our identity before God. One significant consequence of the many that result from our failure to embrace our true identity is that we may lead uncontained, ungrounded, and decentered lives.

Mistaken Identity

When our core identity is not securely rooted in truth—God's truth about who we are—we may find ourselves living our life in a thoroughly ungrounded state, completely missing our center. To the question "Who are we?" Henri Nouwen enumerates the three responses that we typically live but don't necessarily give: "'We are what we do, we are what others say about us, and we are what we have,' or in other words: 'We are our success, we are our popularity, we are our power'" (HN:134).

Nouwen goes on to expose the subtle but severe repercussions of latching on to a warped sense of identity:

> A life without ... a quiet center easily becomes destructive. When we cling to the results of our actions as our only way of self-identification, then we become possessive and defensive and tend to look at our fellow human beings more as enemies to be kept at a distance than as friends with whom we can share the gifts of life. (OS:21)

Many of us have witnessed what a "live wire" that is not grounded looks like. It is skittish because it is uncontained. The same thing characterizes a life that is not centered on a solid sense of identity. A decentered person tends to grasp, to be a taker rather than a giver, to be guarded and reactionary. Such tendencies boil down to a distorted notion of personhood.

Identity Crisis

Who among us has not experienced some version of an identity crisis? Henri Nouwen did—repeatedly, in fact. Again, he discloses the root cause: "The problem is that your identity is hooked up with ... 'I am what I do; I am what people say about me; I am what I have; I am what influence I have'" (B:12). All of these distorted ideas are manifestations of our false selves. They can satisfy us for a while but leave us empty in the end.

> "You are *not* what others, or even you, think about yourself. You are *not* what you do. You are *not* what you have."
>
> —Home Tonight

When we get robbed of our center and no longer feel at home in our inner life, we slowly become stripped of our self-worth. This inevitably leads us to suffer from the terrifying state known as loss of self—which then leads to a loss of hope altogether. As Nouwen lamentingly concludes, "He who has lost his inner self has nothing left to live for" (*AG*:39).

According to Henri Nouwen, if we can single out the major culprit fueling our so-called identity crisis, he believes it is our natural propensity toward self-rejection. "When we have sold our identity to the judges of the world," Nouwen points out, "we are bound to become restless, because of a growing need for affirmation and praise. Indeed, we are tempted to become low-hearted because of a constant self-rejection" (*OS*:20). On this, Nouwen further elaborates:

> Success, popularity, and power can indeed present a great temptation, but their seductive quality comes from the way they are part of the much larger temptation to self-rejection. When we have come to believe in the voices that call us worthless and unlovable, then success, popularity, and power are easily perceived as attractive solutions. (*SD*:30)

Nouwen speaks truthfully from his own personal experience, identifying unashamedly the core of his spiritual conflict as "the struggle against self-rejection, self-contempt, and self-loathing" (*RPS*:107). In the biographical documentary of his life, *Journey of the Heart*, Nouwen recalls the two competing voices he heard while growing up: that of a distant father and that of a nurturing mother. One always urged him to be successful and to be his own independent person whom his father could be proud of, while the other urged him to stay close to God even if he did not accomplish anything of significance in the eyes of the world. In his desire to please his father and win his love and approval,

> "The greatest trap in life is not success, popularity, or power, but self-rejection, doubting who we truly are."
>
> —*Spiritual Direction*

Nouwen strove hard toward his own self-fulfillment and success, only to find himself perennially struggling with self-doubt and rejection. In *The Return of the Prodigal Son*, he poignantly admits to this constant wrestling:

> Over and over again I have left home. I have fled the hands of blessing and run off to faraway places searching for love! This is

the great tragedy of my life and of the lives of so many I meet on
my journey. Somehow I have become deaf to the voice that calls
me the Beloved, have left the only place where I can hear that
voice, and have gone off desperately hoping that I would find
somewhere else what I could no longer find at home. (RPS:39)

Nouwen recognizes that his failure to claim God's first love, along with
that original goodness for himself, led him to lose touch with his own true
self and to follow a destructive path, among the wrong people, in all the
wrong places, in a desperate search for what can only be found in God's
house (RPS:107). Nouwen's insatiable longing for human intimacy drove
him to be especially demanding, clingy, and possessive when it came to
his close friends. This became particularly pronounced in his relationship
with Nathan Ball, his closest coworker at L'Arche Daybreak. The eventual
breakup of their friendship only worsened Nouwen's lingering feeling of
rejection. Coming out of that dark episode in his life, Nouwen realized
that when you demand of the second love what only the first love can
give, you crash and suffer from a massive lack of identity security.

Thus Nouwen does not have any qualms arriving at the sensible con-
clusion that indeed "self-rejection is the greatest enemy of the spiritual life
because it contradicts the sacred voice that calls us the 'Beloved.' Being the
Beloved expresses the core truth of our existence" (LB:28). Everything and
everyone around us is trying to tell us that our belovedness is not true. It's a
huge battle, a spiritual battle, because "it's a fight for [our] identity" (B:20).

Reclaiming Our Center

How then do we aggressively fight this battle? Is there a concrete way that
we can overcome this number-one enemy of ours?

First, Henri Nouwen highlights the power of choice we all possess and
directs our focus toward the spiritual practice of claiming (and reclaiming)
our primal identity as a beloved son or daughter of our personal Creator.
Here he helps put things in the right perspective for us:

Strong emotions, self-rejection, and even self-hatred justifiably
toss you around, but you are free to respond as you will. You are
not what others, or even you, think about yourself. You are *not*
what you do. You are *not* what you have. You are a full member of

the human family, having been known before you were conceived and molded in your mother's womb. In times when you feel bad about yourself, try to choose to remain true to the truth of who you really are. Look in the mirror each day and claim your true identity. Act ahead of your feelings and trust that one day your feelings will match your convictions. Choose now and continue to choose this incredible truth. (HT:50)

Nouwen brings our attention back to the crucial role that solitude plays in our attempt to confront our battle head-on: "In solitude we re-find our center" (CR:23).

Nouwen confidently and repeatedly assures us, "There is in each of us an inner voice of Love that says: 'You are the Beloved of God!'" (SD:28). And based on this solid assurance, he issues a firm admonition we all would do well to heed:

I want you to claim your Belovedness. You don't have to get caught in searches that lead nowhere. Neither do you have to become the victim of a manipulative world or get trapped in any kind of addiction. You can choose to reach out now for true inner freedom and find it ever more fully. (SD:28)

From experience, Nouwen attests, "When I can accept my identity from God and allow him to be the center of my life, I am liberated from compulsion and can move without restraints" (GD:203). To Nouwen, reclaiming our center is tantamount to embracing our real identity in God. This idea is equated with the image of coming home to our true self. In his own words, "Returning, then, is moving toward containment, toward home, holding fast to our true identity as the Beloved of the Divine" (HT:42).

> "There is in each of us an inner voice of Love that says: 'You are the Beloved of God!'"
>
> —Spiritual Direction

Our True Spiritual Identity

Since our life is rooted in our spiritual identity, Henri Nouwen urges us to always "go back to our first love, back regularly to that place of core identity" (SD:34). He prompts us to recall:

Your true identity is as a child of God. This is the identity you have
to accept. Once you have claimed it and settled in it, you can live in
a world that gives you much joy as well as pain. You can receive the
praise as well as the blame that comes to you as an opportunity for
strengthening your basic identity, because the identity that makes
you free is anchored beyond human praise and blame. (IVL:70)

Without any tinge of embarrassment, Nouwen admits to a seemingly
never-ending struggle to appropriate this truth into his own experience.
In fact, it took a close brush with death for Nouwen to allow the truth of
his identity to finally sink deeply into the center of his heart and lead him
to a much fuller embrace of his spiritual status. In *Beyond the Mirror*,
where Nouwen chronicles in detail a near-fatal accident that forced him to
seriously reflect on the sobering issues of life
and death, he proclaims, "I am a child of God,
a brother of Jesus. I am held safe in the intimacy of the divine love" (BM:68).

"Prayer and meditation
are important ...
because in them you
can find your deepest
identity."

—*The Genesee Diary*

It bears noting that nothing short of a
mystical experience disposed Nouwen to
arrive at this bold proclamation. He implies
that there is a correlation between mysticism
and our inner capacity to truly grasp the reality of God's love for us. In
fact, a mystical element is almost required to see through to this incredible
truth of our belovedness in God, which ultimately seals our core identity.
Little wonder that Nouwen defines a true mystic as "a person whose identity is deeply rooted in God's first love" (INJ:28).

Interestingly, we are here reminded of the foundational importance
of our communion with God and how the practice of contemplative
prayer—within the private setting of solitude—figures prominently in
deepening our understanding of our true identity. Indeed, "solitude is the
sacred meeting place, where we are truly ourselves" (CR:30), enabling us
to center our heart and keep reclaiming our identity in God.

As Nouwen puts it, "Contemplative prayer keeps us home, rooted and
safe ... [and] deepens in us the knowledge that we are already free, that
we have already found a place to dwell, that we already belong to God"
(INJ:29). The question of our identity addresses not just who we are in

God but also whose we are. "To whom do we belong?" remains the central point of our spiritual life (*BBL*:31). Ultimately, drawing our identity from God, who is its source, is what makes all the difference in the world when it comes to centering our heart. For God is undeniably our true centerpoint!

For Further Focused Reading

Beloved

Home Tonight: Further Reflections on the Parable of the Prodigal Son

In the Name of Jesus: Reflections on Christian Leadership

Living It Out

1. Spend twenty minutes doing some form of centering prayer, using "beloved" as your sacred word. Sit in silence, suspending your active thoughts. Each time any distractions enter in—and there will be plenty—gently go back to this word to refocus you. Try doing this at least three times this week, and record your thoughts, feelings, and emotions in a journal.

2. You may also wish to try engaging in "breath prayer" using "I am God's Beloved" as a mantra you repeat to yourself, coinciding with your breath, over and over again until the truth of what you are saying settles in, allowing your mind to descend into your heart. Reflect on this exercise and its effect on you.

3. Do a short, private *lectio divina* (contemplative reading) on Song of Solomon 6:3—"I am my beloved's and my beloved is mine." Observe the standard *lectio divina* pattern of reading, reflecting, responding, and resting, but then add "resolving" (living it out). What invitation from the Spirit are you coming away with as you claim your belovedness? How would you incarnate the reality of your true identity in God in your everyday life? What difference does it make for you and the way you relate to others? Journal about it.

Prayer of the Heart

God, my Creator and Designer,

I have tried to live much of my life as somebody else. I have wished for other people's abilities, other people's successes, other people's relationships, and other people's influence. Yet when I am alone and quiet with you, the imaginary person that I have tried to invent for the sake of my own happiness fades away, and it begins to sink in that you never loved that person anyway—for that person never existed in your mind. The person you have loved as your treasured child is this me who sits here with nothing to bring to impress you. The person you love is the one I have been all along yet am only beginning to know.

The more I let you make me into me, the more everything false falls away, and your love becomes my life. May it be so, for the sake of the fulfillment of your love.

Amen.

THREE

Presence

An Attentive Heart

"The more our spiritual sensitivities come to
the surface of our daily lives, the more we will
discover—uncover—a new presence in our lives."
—A Letter of Consolation

P resence is a notable theme in virtually all of Henri Nouwen's writings. He did not merely address the subject thoroughly; he embodied its reality. The people who knew him best characterized him as one who always evoked a powerful sense of presence wherever he was. A careful reading of his works unveils a discernible pattern of presence, neatly organized into a trilogy: focusing inward, outward, and Godward. This is especially evident in *Reaching Out: The Three Movements of the Spiritual Life*, which presents Nouwen's seminal understanding of our integrated life with God. To Nouwen, real presence means the creation of a free, friendly, empty, open, welcoming, and empowering space where we can be present to ourselves, to one another, and to God. We can cultivate this threefold presence, he suggests, through three avenues—solitude, hospitality, and prayer—that correspond to the three focal points.

Presence and Attentiveness

The notion of presence, as far as Nouwen is concerned, is always coupled with his view of attentiveness. By presence, he means "attentiveness to the blessings" that constantly come our way (*LC*:88). Nouwen understands attentiveness as our capacity to both see and listen almost simultaneously and in an all-encompassing manner. In fact, the cultivation of presence is what makes an attentive heart possible. Nouwen recognizes that "something very deep and mysterious, very holy and sacred, is taking place in our lives right where we are, and the more attentive we become the more we will begin to see and hear it" (*LC*:88). From compilations of remembrances about Nouwen, one thing that stands out consistently was his ability to listen with razor-sharp focus and generous attention to the people he was with.

We are not naturally attentive people. To begin with, we are persistently bombarded with every conceivable form of preoccupation and distraction, preventing us from "seeing the truth of our lives, hearing God's voice, and living a spiritual life" (*SD*:19). For us to even recognize and listen with obedience to God's voice, we must build up resistance to all the other voices constantly vying for our attention.

> "Attentiveness helps us look fully at God, to invite God in more completely. It leads us into the depths of God's healing mercies."
>
> —*Turn My Mourning into Dancing*

To live our spiritual life, as Nouwen reminds us, is never an easy task. By way of analogy, he says, "Marble doesn't give way easily, and neither does the human spirit quickly conform to God's design," for the process involves "a struggle to move from *absurd living* to *obedient listening*" (*SD*:17). The truth is, "the ups and downs of our spiritual lives depend on our obedience—that is, our attentive listening—to the movement of the Spirit of God within us," and without this kind of listening, which Nouwen equates with the process of discernment, "our spiritual life eventually becomes subject to the windswept waves of our emotions" (*BJ*:July 26).

Learning to listen attentively as well as obediently requires a conversional movement of sorts:

> The great movement of the spiritual life is from a deaf, nonhearing life to a life of listening. From a life in which we experience ourselves as separated, isolated, and lonely to a life in which we hear the guiding and healing voice of God, who is with us and will never leave us alone. (*D*:4)

But as Nouwen himself is quick to acknowledge, "the many activities in which we are involved, the many concerns that occupy our time, the many sounds that surround us make it hard for us to hear the 'still, small voice' through which God's presence and will are made known" (*D*:4). These are some of the real barriers to attentive listening that we confront again and again.

A listening heart, as Nouwen describes it, is "a heart in which we stand open to God with all of our questions, with all that we are, and with all that we have" (*SD*:72). In other words, it is a heart that is poised to be openly present—inwardly, outwardly, and Godwardly.

Inward Presence

We are a distracted people immersed in a noisy world. It is hard to see or hear anything with clarity and be present to oneself with all the static we are subjected to day in and day out. An even more challenging task than ridding ourselves of exterior noises is the achievement of what Henri Nouwen refers to as "inner silence, a silence of the heart" (*OH*:36). He equates this state with the idea of being present and at home with oneself. He offers us a glimpse of how this scenario might look:

> To be calm and quiet by yourself ... means being fully awake and following with close attention every move going on inside of you.... It offers the freedom to stroll through your own inner yard and to rake up the leaves and clear the paths so you can easily find the way to your heart. Perhaps there will be fear and uncertainty when you first come upon this "unfamiliar terrain," but slowly and surely you will discover an order and familiarity which deepens your longing to stay at home with yourself. (*OH*:39)

Many of us do not experience the sense of at-homeness that Nouwen speaks about because we are always meandering somewhere else. We are not present to ourselves, and consequently, we are hardly present to our own experience of the moment.

The important question we need to address is how to cultivate this inward presence that will enable us to possess an attentive heart—a heart that empowers us to see and hear clearly the reality of God in us and around us. Henri Nouwen leads us back to the foundational spiritual discipline of solitude. He assures us that "once we have committed our-selves to spending time in solitude, we develop an attentiveness to God's voice in us" (*MTN*:72). Nouwen is convinced that "solitude is the quiet place of listening" (*CR*:23), and "it is in the listening that God becomes present and heals" (*BH*:47). Nouwen is certain that

> every time you listen with great attentiveness to the voice that calls you the Beloved, you will discover within yourself a desire to hear that voice longer and more deeply. It is like discovering a well in the desert. Once you have touched wet ground, you want to dig deeper. (*LB*:31)

In solitude, "we can pay attention to our inner self" (*RO*:41), and there we find ourselves opening up in order to listen to our heart, knowing that it is there that Jesus, who dwells in the very depths of our heart, speaks most intimately to us (*LM*:84). Moreover, through the practice of contemplative prayer, we are enabled to "'see' the living God dwelling in our own hearts." As Nouwen further explains, "Careful attentiveness to One who makes a home in the privileged center of our being gradually leads to recognition" (*CR*:100). Thus it is "by being awake to this God within," through contemplation, that we end up "participating in the divine self-recognition" (*CR*:101).

"In solitude we can become present to ourselves."

—*Reaching Out*

In more ways than one, inward presence intersects with Godward presence. Essentially, when we become present to ourselves, we also become present to God, who is present in us. This is what allows us to see and know God even as we likewise see and know ourselves more deeply. Henri Nouwen explains the intertwining dynamics this way:

> Solitude, silence, and prayer are often the best ways to self-knowledge. Not because they offer solutions for the complexity of our lives but because they bring us in touch with our sacred cen-ter, where God dwells. That sacred center may not be analyzed. It is the place of adoration, thanksgiving, and praise. (*BJ*:Mar 22)

The inward practice of presence through solitude facilitates our expe-rience of double-seeing (seeing God and self) and double-knowing

(knowing God and self), which then leads us to an ever-deepening and well-integrated sense of wholeness and holiness in our life.

Outward Presence

Presence in an outward sense means being with, to, and for the "other" in an attentive way. Cultivation of this type of presence requires that we learn how to be a hospitable "soul host" to other people, strangers and non-strangers alike. By being hospitable Nouwen means the ability to see and listen to others hospitably—with generous spaciousness. Such expression of hospitality is a ministry in and of itself. Those closest to Nouwen, including the people he ministered to in his various roles—whether as spiritual friend, guide, mentor, or spiritual director—all testify to Nouwen's powerful capacity to be available and present to all kinds of people. He, by all accounts, embodied what a hospitable soul host is about. I elaborate on the subject of hospitality and space in part III. For now, we will focus on hospitality within the confines of attentive presence.

This kind of hospitality calls for creative listening. Henri Nouwen submits, "Listening is an art that must be developed, not a technique that can be applied as a monkey wrench to nuts and bolts. It needs the full and real presence of people to each other," as beyond doubt, it is "one of the highest forms of hospitality" (*RO*:95). Listening is a caring way of being a hospitable presence to the other whose life intersects with one's own, as Nouwen illustrates:

> Listening is a very active awareness of the coming together of two lives. When I listen, I listen not only to a story, but also with a story. It is exactly against the background of my own limited story that I discover the uniqueness of the story I am privileged to hear. It is precisely with my own articulate awareness of the piece of the living mosaic that I represent that I can be surprised, sadly or gladly, and can respond from the center of my own life. (*SC*:36)

Practicing true hospitality calls for a balanced employment of what Nouwen refers to as the twin dynamics of receptivity and confrontation.

Receptivity has to do with inviting people into our world on their own terms and not according to ours. It means receiving others without the imposition of our viewpoint or way of living as a condition for extending our hospitality (*RO*:98). To truly listen in a hospitable, welcoming way is to refuse to act as a teacher but rather to submit oneself as a student of the one we are receiving in our midst (see *SC*:34–35).

Nouwen points out that there is also a flip side to receptivity characterized by an unambiguous and articulate sense of presence, which is expressed through confrontation. Confrontation is a form of witness characterized by a refusal to hide ourselves behind neutrality but instead a willingness to open up our ideas, opinions, and lifestyle clearly and distinctly without ever imposing them on others. A careful balance between the two is in order. As Nouwen rightly warns, "Receptivity without confrontation leads to a bland neutrality that serves nobody. Confrontation without receptivity leads to an oppressive aggression which hurts everybody" (*RO*:98–99). Thus real hospitable presence invariably involves the capacity to receive as well as confront.

Moreover, to be a welcoming, hospitable presence toward others presupposes that the host feels at home in her *own* house. For, as Nouwen makes clear, a true host is somebody who offers others space devoid of any fear—a space "where we can listen to our own inner voices and find our own personal way of being human" (*RO*:102). Even more importantly, a good host is one who understands the paradox of hospitality—that "poverty makes a good host"—and knows how to properly employ an inner disposition of friendliness along with a stance of nondefensiveness toward others. Here Nouwen identifies two forms of poverty that are of critical importance to listening to and receiving others freely: poverty of mind and poverty of heart (*RO*:103).

> "Healing means ... the creation of an empty but friendly space where those who suffer can tell their story to someone who can listen with real attention."
>
> —*Reaching Out*

Poverty of mind is fundamentally a spiritual attitude of spaciousness and receptivity to others without the compelling need to always know and be right about everything. Nouwen says that "someone who is filled with ideas, concepts, opinions, and convictions cannot be a good host. There is no inner space to listen, no openness to discover the gift of the other" (*RO*:103). Similarly, poverty of heart is a learned capacity to welcome other people's unique and varied experiences as precious gifts to receive wholeheartedly. Henri Nouwen is right: "When our heart is filled with prejudices, worries, jealousies, there is little room for a stranger. In a fearful environment it is not easy to keep our hearts open to the wide range of human experiences" (*RO*:106–107). Genuine hospitality is, after all, a very inclusive endeavor that generously flows toward others through our authentic exercise of outward presence.

Godward Presence

The final kind of attentive presence is directed to the Divine Presence. If inward presence is practiced via solitude and outward presence via hospitality, Godward presence is practiced through the avenue of prayer, specifically communing prayer—perhaps the highest form of prayer—which focuses intimately on our union with God. To Nouwen, "prayer is the expression of a most intimate relationship," and therefore the language itself seems reserved within the vocabulary of "love, lovers, art, and artists" (*RO*:115).

As a Dutchman, Nouwen always had a fascination with wagon wheels and their wide rims, wooden spokes, and big hubs. They all symbolize for Nouwen what a life lived from the center is all about—a life glued at the hub, where one remains in touch with all the spokes at once. To him, the hub—"the center of all energy and movement"—represents his own heart, God's heart, and the heart of the world. Nouwen was convinced that the closer he was to the hub of life, the closer he was to all that gathers energy and strength from this center. Thus, he thought of the act of prayer as a determined movement to the very center of all life and love (*HN*:23). To commune with God in prayer, therefore, is to be intimately present to the Source.

This, to Nouwen, is "one of the most concrete ways to reach out to God from the center of our innermost self" where, according to Theophan the Recluse, we allow our mind to descend into our heart, "and there stand before the face of the Lord, ever present,

> "When we pray, we enter into the presence of God whose name is God-with-us."
>
> —*Here and Now*

all seeing" within us (*RO*:145). When we pray accordingly and direct our minds and hearts with our fullest attention, we can listen attentively to the voice of love, "to the One who addresses us here and now" (*HN*:20–21).

To learn to be attentively present to the ultimate Presence through prayer is what enables us to exercise discernment in our spiritual life. This involves the increasing capacity to "listen to God, to pay attention to God's active presence, and to obey God's prompting, direction, leadings, and guidance" (*SD*:5). As I mentioned in the introduction, the familiar Emmaus Road story (Luke 24:13–36) has powerful eucharistic symbolism for Nouwen. It is also a wonderful and compelling illustration of what it means to be present. Henri Nouwen highlights the four critical movements in the story with corresponding practical applications:

> Discerning the divine presence through scripture reading (*lectio divina*), staying with Christ (abiding in his presence in prayer) in the breaking of bread (Eucharist), and remembering Jesus (*anamnesis*) results in the burning heart experience (of divine memory, or *memoria Christi*). (*D*:122; see pp. 115–122 for broader context)

Although Nouwen himself did not incorporate the ideas of an attentive heart and inward, outward, and Godward presence in his commentary of the Emmaus passage, it is evident that the account shows how the two disciples embodied these things. They were inwardly present in that they were self-aware enough to recognize their burning heart sensation while Jesus was expounding on the scripture; they were outwardly present in the way they extended hospitality to, with, and for Jesus, the "stranger," insisting that he stay with them for the night; and they were Godwardly present when they finally recognized the real presence in Jesus through the breaking of bread.

Presence sets the stage for the cultivation of an attentive heart, a heart endowed with the inner capacity to see and listen. The same attentive heart is what makes possible a deepening process of discernment in our spiritual life.

For Further Focused Reading

Discernment: Reading the Signs of Daily Life

Here and Now: Living in the Spirit

Reaching Out: The Three Movements of the Spiritual Life

Living It Out

1. In *solitude*, we become present to ourselves by creating a space in our hearts to see and know who we truly are in God. Jot

down some practical ways you can claim and reclaim your true identity in God through your own cultivation of inward presence and intentional engagement in solitude, silence, and contemplative prayer.

2. Through *hospitality*, we become present to, with, and for others by creating a space in us and for them so that we can become a more hospitable host. Ponder and then apply the various ways you can exercise hospitality by employing what Nouwen calls "poverty of mind and poverty of heart" with your existing community or small group.

3. In *prayer*, we become present to the Divine Presence who is ever present to us. We create a space for God in our hearts so that we can see and know God more experientially. How can you create a space for God so that you can actually be present to the Presence? What kind of communing prayer will enhance your experience of Godward presence? Engage in it throughout the week. Record your thoughts and insights in your journal.

Prayer of the Heart

God who is with me,

Help me to be here with you, as you are here with me, right now. I do not need to be anywhere else, anyone else, nor do I need anything else to be more fully with you. Open these ears that you have given me to hear the sounds that are really around me. Open these eyes that you have given me to see this moment as it actually is. And as you teach me to see and hear this life that you have so generously gifted to me, may I offer that kind of attentive presence to those with whom my path crosses. As I find myself here with you, show me how to recognize your presence here with my brothers and sisters, so that this longing that is so deep within us can be touched—that we may be one as you are one.

Amen.

Part II

Community
A Life Shared

"The Christian community is a community of
people who remind each other who they truly are—
the beloved of God."
—Beloved

"Community is first of all a quality of the heart.
It grows from the spiritual knowledge that we are
alive not for ourselves but for one another."
—Bread for the Journey

"Community is first and foremost a gift of the Holy
Spirit.... It is the God-within who brings us into
communion with each other and makes us one."
—Behold the Beauty of the Lord

"When morning came, he called his disciples to him and chose twelve of them, whom he also designated apostles."

—Luke 6:13 NIV

We know from the different Gospel accounts that each time Jesus emerged from his private communion with God, he did not stay detached but rather reengaged with people even more deeply. Luke's Gospel, in particular, tells us that after an all-night immersion in God's presence in solitude, Jesus gathered to him his newfound, newly formed community of apostles, with whom he would stay intimately connected and journey along until his time on earth was up.

Henri Nouwen directs our awareness to the fact that communion creates and builds community "because the God living in us makes us recognize the God in our fellow humans. We cannot see God in the other person. Only God in us can see God in the other person.... Our participation in the inner life of God leads us to a new way of participation in each other's lives" (*BH*:75–76). Moreover, "it is precisely in communion with God through prayer that we discover the call to community" (*SL*:33). "Solitude always calls us to community," he assures us (*SD*:112). Why? Because through our time of solitude, we come to recognize again and again that we are not alone but part of a human family—that in our spiritual life and journey, we are designed to live and operate communally. Our life as a whole is never meant to be a solitary existence. Intuitively, we understand that "we cannot live a spiritual life alone. The life of the Spirit is like a seed that needs fertile ground to grow. This fertile ground includes not only a good inner disposition, but also a supportive milieu" (*HN*:95). Just as we were created for communion with God, we were also created for community by the Triune God, who ultimately embodies eternal communion and community.

39

For Henri Nouwen, community represents our "spiritual home" where, as a gathered people, we manifest "a way of living and relating" in such a way that together we can confidently "proclaim the truth that we are the beloved sons and daughters of God" (SD:113). In direct conjunction with our communion with God, here is how Nouwen grasps the interrelationship between solitude and community:

> Solitude greeting solitude, that's what community is all about.... Our solitude roots us in our own hearts. Instead of making us yearn for company that will offer us immediate satisfaction, solitude makes us claim our center and empowers us to call others to claim theirs. Our various solitudes are like strong, straight pillars that hold up the roof of our communal house. (BJ:Jan 22)

Community is like whispering to one another, "I am the Beloved; you are the Beloved. Together we can build a home ... and create space for God and for the children of God" (SL:36). Among other things, this means that as we increasingly become grounded in our belovedness before God, we also grow in our secure capacity to be givers rather than takers who suck the life out of the community because of our own unmet needs.

Community and Spirit

The foundation upon which our community of faith is built is none other than God dwelling within us all. The Spirit is responsible for fashioning this community, which Nouwen distinguishes as an entity "not built upon mutual compatibility, shared affection, or common interests, but upon having received the same divine breath, having been given a heart set aflame by the same divine fire and having been embraced by the same divine love" (BBL:65). The God-within is the one gathering us together into communion and bringing us into unity.

> "Solitude always strengthens community."
> —Bread for the Journey

Elsewhere, Nouwen reinforces this same conviction by reiterating that "the basis of community is not primarily our ideas, feelings, and emotions about each other but our common search for God. When we keep our minds and hearts directed toward God, we will come more fully 'together'" (GD:213). Thus all of us who are part of the community are brought into a "new unity [that] invites us to make that new unity a source of joy and hope for each other and for others as well" (LC:27). Nouwen puts it this way: "A life well held is indeed a life for others" (CDC:58).

The quality of community that Henri Nouwen has in mind is one that is decidedly others-centered. He debunks the often distorted notions of community associated with "sectarian exclusivity, in-group language, self-satisfied isolation, and romantic naiveté" (BJ:Jan 23). Nouwen is persuaded that true spiritual community exists beyond the mere well-being of its members and that this Spirit-formed organism is "called to make God's love visible, and thus work for the liberation of the world" (BBL:67, 75).

Disciplines of Community Life

Henri Nouwen is convinced that every form of community has to be governed by certain habits or disciplines to which the members commit themselves. On this aspect, he sets forth the twofold discipline of forgiveness coupled with confession, and celebration, without which, he insists, no community can possibly be sustained (SL:36). "We need ... a community in which confession and celebration are always present together" (CDC:60). Both dynamics must be a habitual practice embedded into the very fabric of the community.

> "Community is like a large mosaic ... of little people who together make God visible in the world."
>
> —Can You Drink the Cup?

Learning to exercise confession and forgiveness is first and foremost. In fact, "offering and receiving forgiveness is where community begins to be created. Community forms when we come together in a forgiving and unde-manding way" (SL:38). A healthy and robust community life requires a prevailing attitude of forgiveness. "Forgiveness holds us together through good and bad times, and it allows us to grow in mutual love" (BJ:Jan 24). And what must we constantly forgive? Nouwen issues a much-needed reminder that "we need to forgive one another for not being God" (SD:120). We are only too painfully aware that even the best of us are bound to fail each other time and again by virtue of our own inherent imperfections.

Celebration follows forgiveness and is a tangible manifestation of love (see SD:123–124). Our community serves as the perfect context to call forth and rejoice in each other's giftedness. "In community we are leaders from the place of our gifts and followers from the place of other people's gifts" (*SL*:40–41). We have need of each other all the time. Always we function as interdependent members who can rely on one another through our shared human triumphs and travails. Nouwen offers us a realistic portrait of community life:

> Community is a fellowship of people who do not hide their joys and sorrows but make them visible to each other in a gesture of hope. In community we say: "Life is full of gains and losses, joys and sorrows, ups and downs—but we do not have to live it alone. We want to drink our cup together and thus celebrate the truth that the wounds of our individual lives, which seem intolerable when lived alone, become sources of healing when we live them as part of a fellowship of mutual care." (*CDC*:57)

In view of this hopeful scenario, Nouwen urges us to do the very thing he kept reminding himself: "Keep returning to those to whom you belong and who keep you in the light. It is that light that you desire to bring into the darkness. You do not have to fear anyone as long as you remain safely anchored in your community. Then you can carry the light far and wide" (*IVL*:46). Ultimately, Nouwen tells us, community is for others' sake—never exclusive but always inclusive.

> "Community cultivates that mutual vulnerability in which we forgive each other and celebrate each other's gifts."
>
> —*A Spirituality of Living*

Henri Nouwen concludes, "With forgiveness and celebration, community becomes the place where we call forth the gifts of other people, lift them up, and say, 'You are the beloved daughter and the beloved son. With you I am well pleased'" (*SD*:124). These twin dynamics are what sustain the life of every community.

Community and Prayer

Just as prayer and communion are intertwined, so are community and prayer. Nouwen reckons prayer as the breath of our life, as it pervades all aspects of our existence. "It is the unceasing recognition that God is wherever we are, always inviting us to come closer and to celebrate the divine gift of being alive" (*OH*:122). In prayer we allow the life-giving Spirit of God to penetrate every corner of our being (*SJ*:5).

It is through prayer, Nouwen believes, that Christian community gets created and expressed. Prayer is foremost our recognition of the very presence of God in the midst of God's people and, as such, our recognition of the presence of community itself. Prayer serves as the community's native language. Nouwen expounds on why this is the case: "In prayer the nature of the community becomes visible because in prayer we direct ourselves to the one who forms the community. We do not pray to each other, but together we pray to God, who calls us and makes us into a new people" (*RO*:156).

> "Praying is not one of the many things the community does. Rather, it is its very being."
>
> —*Reaching Out*

If we were to single out the one overriding discipline of a spiritual community, it would be prayer, which enables us to be vigilant to the very presence of the Holy Spirit, "who cries out 'Abba, Father,' among us and thus prays from the center of our common life" (*MTN*:87).

In our community of faith, we find the climate and even the support we need to deepen our prayer lives (*RO*:152). Individually and communally, we look for the active presence of the Holy Spirit as we endeavor to pray.

> When we have heard God's voice in our solitude we will also hear it in our life together. When we have heard him in our fellow human beings, we will also hear him when we are with him alone. Whether in solitude or community, whether alone or with others, we are called to live obedient lives, that is, lives of unceasing prayer—"unceasing" not because of the many prayers we say but because of our alertness to the unceasing prayer of God's Spirit within and among us. (*MTN*:91–92)

Nouwen visualizes communal and individual prayer like two folded hands that are connected to each other; they are inextricably bound together. He notes the attendant consequences when the two are separated from each other: "Without community, individual prayer easily degenerates into egocentric and eccentric behavior, but without individual prayer, the prayer of the community quickly becomes a meaningless routine" (*RO*:158).

As a community of prayer, with bonded hearts, we seek to deepen our sense of togetherness, while operating from the standpoint of mutuality based on our commonality, and reach out to the larger community in deep solidarity with those to whose hearts we feel strongly connected.

Personal Ponderings

1. What kind of a community am I a part of? How would I describe it? Do I feel like I truly belong there? If I were to name our community's reason for being, what would that be? What are some of the characteristics of my community that make me want to stick it out there?

2. Does my community practice the twofold dynamic of forgiveness and celebration? As a member, do I engage in them myself? In reflecting on them, what difference does it make, really? Have I personally experienced a difference between a community that practices forgiveness and celebration and a community that doesn't?

3. As I ponder my own spiritual journey, how has community life enriched my relationship with God? How have I experienced transformation as a result of my communal engagement? How have I personally contributed to the building up of my community? As a community, are we a credible witness of God's love to the watching world? In what specific ways have we demonstrated the reality of God to those outside of our circle? Can I claim that we are genuinely a community that cares for others?

FOUR

Togetherness

A Bonded Heart

"Through the discipline of community we
discover a place for God in our life together."
—*Making All Things New*

In life it is comforting to take into account the assurance that we are never alone, even if sometimes we feel otherwise. The truth is, "being human means being together" (*OH*:91). Since God designed us for community, our existence—and even our life calling—is never meant to be a solitary experience: "We are always called together" (*CR*:19). By divine intention, we are supposed to hold on tightly to a healthy sense of togetherness, for this is naturally what makes for a strong and thriving community.

For Henri Nouwen, community is our coming together as a people united by a bond of love. Appealing to his favorite wagon wheel symbol, he explains the communal dynamics of our being bound together:

> God is the hub of the wheel of life. The closer we come to God the closer we come to each other. The basis of community is not primarily our ideas, feelings, and emotions about each other but our common search for God. When we keep our minds and hearts directed toward God, we will come more fully "together." (*GD*:213)

Our sense of togetherness, however, goes beyond the idea of just living and working together. "It is a bond of the heart that has no physical limitations. Indeed it is candles burning in different places of the world, all praying the same silent prayer of friendship and love" (*SJ*:29). The bondedness of a true community exists at the heart level, with love holding it together.

Henri Nouwen was familiar with this level of bonding from the relationship he enjoyed with his mother before she passed away. In the book he wrote in memory of her, *In Memoriam*, Nouwen fondly reminisced about the joy they both felt in simply being together: "We were together in a moment of truth, a moment we wanted to taste together" (*IM*:17–19). And in that state of togetherness, he claimed to have been surrounded by strength like they had never before experienced. Isn't this type of togetherness supposed to provide our community—regardless of size—a similar quality of experience?

In Nouwen's vivid description of his intimate relationship with his mother, we witness in transparent ways their bonded hearts: "It was the joy of feeling a great love binding us together, a love ... given us and which was not going to be taken away from us" (*IM*:36). To him, the sense of togetherness they had was a graced space of rest that was "more given than made" (*IM*:38). None of it felt forced. The whole experience was spontaneous and free. Nouwen recounts:

> The prayers we said together became the place where we could be together without fear or apprehension. They became like a safe house in which we could dwell, communicating things to each other without having to grope for inadequate, self-made expressions. (*IM*:38)

Nouwen's poignant recollections of bonding in *In Memoriam* are not exclusive to the relationship between a parent and a child. Neither are they limited to the context of a family or even to friendships. They can be realized on a larger scale within any community setting where an authentic sense of togetherness is lived out with true abandon.

Togetherness in the Eucharist

The role of the Eucharist is uppermost in Nouwen's experience, and it necessarily includes the realm of community for him. Nouwen is convinced that "the Eucharist was and is the center of the fellowship of those who put their trust in Jesus" (*LM*:35). For Nouwen, "the sacrament of love ... and the self-surrendering love which we encounter in the Eucharist is the source of true Christian community" (*LM*:48). In the ten years that Nouwen ministered at L'Arche Daybreak, his celebration of the Eucharist figured prominently in the life of the community. Despite the fact that Daybreak was decidedly interfaith and openly inclusive in its thrust, its community life was heavily influenced by Nouwen's conviction as a Catholic priest that the regular gathering at the Lord's table served as a tangible expression of communal love. Nouwen opened the table to everyone regardless of their faith tradition, a practice that was clearly a departure from the official Catholic position of closed communion. Nouwen was convinced that "in the Eucharist God's love is most concretely made present. Jesus has not only become human, he has also become bread and wine in order that, through eating and drinking, God's love might become our own" (*LM*:62).

The Eucharist is not only the sacrament of love but also the sacrament of unity, because "it makes us into one body." It is not simply a place to celebrate our unity; the Eucharist itself forges unity in that by eating from the same bread and drinking from the same cup, we become present to each other as members of the same body (*BJ*:Oct 8). Each time we assemble for the Eucharist, we do so in the name of Jesus, who calls us together to remember his death and resurrection through the breaking of the bread. The Eucharist as the sacrament of

> "The Eucharist not only signifies unity but also creates it."
>
> —*Bread for the Journey*

Christ's presence within and among us "creates the one body of Christ, living in the world as a vibrant sign of unity and community" (*BJ*: Oct 9–10). There is no togetherness like the one we experience—in an almost mystical sense—when we come to the table as a community to partake of the spiritual food and drink offered by our Lord Jesus Christ, who called us to be his Body.

Dynamics of Togetherness

Henri Nouwen's concept of togetherness as a community veers away from our typical associations of togetherness being sentimental, romantic, or homey. On the contrary, he clarifies that this kind of togetherness, particularly of a Christian community, is "a being-gathered-in-displacement." Such is the conundrum of community—the rather strange reality that we are gathered together knowing and willing that we can displace ourselves at any time when called to do so (*C*:63). In accordance with the example of our displaced Lord, who willingly gave up his heavenly abode to live humbly with mortals like us, voluntary displacement, Nouwen points out, is a true mark of discipleship. "It is in following our displaced Lord," he adds, "that the Christian community is formed" (*C*:64–66). As Nouwen concludes, "The Christian community gathers in displacement and in so doing discovers and proclaims a new way of being together" (*C*:75).

"The togetherness of the Christian community ... grows from a deep sense of being called together to make God's compassion visible in the concreteness of everyday living." Voluntary displacement "is meaningful only when it gathers together in a new way" (*C*:76). Nouwen views displacement, therefore, as inauthentic when it does not result in a community being brought more tightly together. He experienced firsthand the resultant blessings usually accompanying the reality of displacement. Actually, in addition to voluntary displacement, Nouwen was also subjected to involuntary displacement when he pulled out temporarily from the community fourteen months after settling down at L'Arche Daybreak. This was triggered by his nervous breakdown resulting from a sudden interruption of his close relationship with his colleague Nathan Ball. His seven-month absence from the community proved so healing for Nouwen, that when he came back, he felt like a different person, with more life to give to the community. What seemed at first to be an experience of liability both for Nouwen and the community turned out to be an asset for community members, who became recipients of even more abundant blessings flowing out of Nouwen's revived soul. Thus, regardless of what kind of displacement occurs in a community setting, there is always the prospect of a new way of being together as a re-gathered community to which we can look forward. This hope is always there to welcome and greet us.

> "The Christian community is not driven together but drawn together."
>
> —*Compassion*

A New Way of Being Together

Voluntary displacement can lead us to a new kind of togetherness, whereby we can acknowledge our similarities in common vulnerability, uncover our unique talents as gifts for the building up of our community, and respond to God's calling, which represents our genuine vocation (C:85). Henri Nouwen is right in saying that "we discover how much we have to give to each other" the more we gather together in such common vulnerability. This new way of being together essentially means "that our unique talents are no longer objects of competition but elements of community, no longer qualities that divide but gifts that unite" (C:78–79).

In community, our similarities as well as our uniqueness can be affirmed simultaneously. Nouwen expounds on the broad implications of this truth:

> When we unmask the illusion that a person is the difference she or he makes, we can come together on the basis of our common human brokenness and our common need for healing. Then we also can come to the marvelous realization that hidden in the ground on which we walk together are the talents that we can offer to each other. (C:79)

Indeed, community "leads to the discovery or rediscovery of each other's hidden talents and makes us realize our own unique contribution to the common life" (C:79). It is precisely in our experience of togetherness that we have ample opportunities to "call forth the hidden gifts in each other and receive them in gratitude as valuable contributions to our life in community" (C:81). Instead of elevating our individual differences—which can readily fuel competition among us—we recognize and celebrate these differences as potential contributions to an even richer life together, thus enabling us to more clearly hear our holy call to community (C:82).

It is valuable to be reminded that in our endeavor to form a Christian community, "we come together not because of similar experiences, knowledge, problems, color, or sex, but because

"The Christian community ... is the place where individual gifts can be called forth and put into service for all."

—*Compassion*

we have been called together by the same Lord" (C:82). As Nouwen is careful to point out, "Life in community is a response to a vocation. God calls us together into one people fashioned in the image of Christ. It is by Christ's vocation that we are gathered" (C:83). Our life of togetherness is bonded and sealed by the unmistakable sense of calling we receive from no less than the three-in-one God who is forever a community.

For Further Focused Reading

Clowning in Rome: Reflections on Solitude, Celibacy, Prayer, and Contemplation

Compassion: A Reflection on the Christian Life

In Memoriam

Living It Out

1. Identify a particular community with which you are actively affiliated. As you visualize the faces of the various members you know, jot down on a piece of paper the talents and gifts of each that come to mind. Take time to celebrate each person's unique contribution to the community by breathing a word of gratitude to God on his or her behalf and perhaps, as you feel prompted, send a note of appreciation to some of them—in whatever way you deem appropriate.

2. The next time you celebrate the Eucharist, pause for a brief contemplative moment and offer thanksgiving to God (that's exactly what the word "Eucharist" means) for the sacrament of love and unity you enjoy together with your community, savoring the very presence of one another as members of the same body.

3. Personalizing this theme of togetherness, ask yourself: What is it that I bring to my community that only I can deliver? How and when do I plan on blessing the members of my community in a manner that serves to strengthen our way of being together? Try to be practical and creative at the same time.

Prayer of the Heart

Our Father,

Take us ever farther into you, so that we can find ourselves and one another. When I am alone with you, help me to see the incomparable gift of my brothers' and sisters' presence in my life. When we are together in community, use each of us to shape one another in love so we can become truly and fully who you created us to be. And when we gather around your family table, make us one in you through the body and blood given so freely to all of us.

Amen.

FIVE

Mutuality

A Common Heart

"It is precisely in the moments when we are most
human, most in touch with what binds us together,
that we discover the hidden paths of life."
—*Compassion*

Amid the diversity of our community life, we are afforded opportunities to celebrate not only the reality of our stark differences, but
more so our vast commonalities as a gathered people. We possess a common heart that beats with one accord. This manifests itself concretely in
an abiding sense of mutuality. In Henri Nouwen's understanding, "It is
among the most common human experiences ... that we touch the mystery of human life.... In many different ways ... what is most universal is
also most personal" (*IM*:10). Our varying expressions of mutuality form
and inform the shape and quality of our communal undertaking.

As we have seen, a community's calling is always a common calling—
a reality made even more apparent when we contemplate it while in our
state of solitude. For in solitude we see with appreciation our oneness
amid our uniqueness, our unity in diversity within and among our community. Since God calls us as a people, it makes sense that "our own
individual calling can only be seen as a particular manifestation of the
calling of the community to which we belong" (*CR*:21). This explains in

part why we choose to align ourselves with certain kinds of community. Usually it is because of the compatibility—and mutuality—of calling that exists between us and our chosen community. In this sense we naturally support each other in the pursuit of our common calling.

Mutuality in Ministry

Ministry within the context of community is certainly a mutual experience (*INJ*:40). Henri Nouwen clarifies, "We are sinful, broken, vulnerable people who need as much care as anyone we care for" (*INJ*:43–44). Mutuality ought not to be seen as a weakness and a form of role confusion. It behooves us to minister to each other despite our socially designated roles or ranks, regardless of the artificial hierarchal structure we tend to impose on each other. In God's eyes, we are all the same—whether as leaders or followers. In community as in ministry such distinctions automatically collapse in the face of our common need. All of us need God desperately in the same way that we need every single person in our community.

As ministers—professional and lay—we are vulnerable servants who need people as much as people need us (*INJ*:44–45). It is never a one-way street. Ministers not only minister but allow themselves to be ministered to as well. We find the Epistles replete with passages that address mutuality in ministry within the context of community life and, more specifically, our church life. As believers in Christ, we owe each other—and in fact share with each other—the common responsibility to fulfill the job of "one another-ing": admonishing one another (Romans 15:7), encouraging one another (1 Thessalonians 5:11), and bearing one another's burdens (Galatians 6:2), to name just a few.

"What is most universal is also most personal."

—*In Memoriam*

Mutuality in Confession and Forgiveness

Our mutuality is sustained in tangible ways through the exercise of confession and forgiveness among ourselves (*INJ*:65). All of us have a vital accountability to confess, and all of us have an obligation to forgive. The dynamics of confession and forgiveness are "the concrete forms in which we sinful people love one another" (*INJ*:46). Nouwen states that "what makes a Christian community is a life of mutual confession and forgiveness in the name of Jesus" wherein the members demonstrate a willingness to live in shared openness and transparency (*PW*:102). Through this process we are reminded of the sobering truth that in our humanity we are no different from everyone else. As a result, we can "allow ourselves to lay down our heavy armor and come together in a mutual vulnerability" (*OS*:42). Henri Nouwen admonishes ministers to have the humble openness and willingness to admit their own neediness and brokenness in order to overcome the snare of what he calls "individual heroism" (*INJ*:45). Moreover, they too need to be ready to ask forgiveness as necessary from the people they minister to, so as to ensure that their ministry operates within the context of the healing and reconciling presence of Jesus.

Nouwen reminds us that there is no need to compare or compete with each other. We can and must be able to depend on each other as members of the same community. Daring to become reliant on the other means "allowing the other to become part of our lives" and having the inner freedom to admit to the other, "Without you I wouldn't be who I am" (*BJ*:Apr 4). Even better, as a community we can live and work interdependently with each other, which is the primary way God designed our communal life to function in the first place.

> "Ministry is not only a communal experience, it is also a mutual experience."
>
> —*In the Name of Jesus*

Henri Nouwen observes that the people who take part in a community where confession and forgiveness are consistently practiced tend to live eucharistically—that is, with a life of overflowing gratitude. They are thankful that they are not alone; they always have each other to lean on. To Nouwen, "the greatest service we can offer each other is mutual support in our conversion from resentment to gratitude" (*PW*:117). In our commonality, we have reason to celebrate our equality; in our differences, we have reason to appreciate our complementarity. Such a perspective eliminates the tendency for resentment to overpower us, allowing instead for an attitude of thankfulness to take over.

Mutuality in Giving and Receiving

Communal relationship is defined by a give-and-take stance, where support is generously extended and openly received by everyone in the community. As needy people, we give as we ourselves are willing to receive in the process. Nouwen offers this admonition as he envisions a continuous mutuality between giving and receiving:

> Let's never give anything without asking ourselves what we are receiving from those to whom we give, and let's never receive anything without asking what we have to give to those from whom we receive. (*BJ*:Apr 2)

To emphasize this dynamic interplay further, Nouwen notes that while giving is vital in that "without giving there is no brotherhood and sisterhood," receiving is equally important because "by receiving we reveal to the givers that they have gifts to offer." He notes, "Sometimes it is only in the eyes of the receivers that givers discover their gifts" (*BJ*:Apr 1).

Mutuality and Complementarity

We are given a wonderful glimpse of the outworking of mutuality and complementarity in Nouwen's own life, particularly while he was living and ministering at L'Arche Daybreak, an ecumenical community where people with disabilities and their assistants live together according to the gospel. It was at Daybreak that he met Nathan Ball and Sue Mosteller, two of the most significant people on his own communal journey.

In the diary of his final year, *Sabbatical Journey*, Nouwen says of these two friends, "The moments of ecstasy and agony connected with both of them mark my nine years at Daybreak" (*SJ*:7).

"The greatest service we can offer each other is mutual support."

—*Peacework*

Through them he came to discover how friendship does not happen by itself but requires concentrated effort—something never to take for granted: "Friendship requires trust, patience, attentiveness, courage, repentance, forgiveness, celebration, and most of all faithfulness" (*SJ*:7). If anything, Nouwen's friendships with Ball and Mosteller were characterized by mutual sharing, mutual support, and mutual conformity or alignment in life.

Mutuality with Nathan Ball

Nouwen and Ball first crossed each other's paths in France while Nouwen was discerning a possible call to serve at L'Arche. In one of his diary entries in *The Road to Daybreak*, Nouwen recalls with fondness the birth of his new friendship with Ball and the prospect of sustaining a lasting relationship of mutual love and support with him: "Someone is emerging who is becoming a friend, a new companion in life, a new presence that will last wherever I will go" (RD:99). What drew them together almost immediately was their mutual need for friendship and the way they complemented one another in their common pursuit to live the spiritual life faithfully. Despite a considerable gap in age—Ball being much younger—theirs was an egalitarian relationship of colleagues.

To Ball, Nouwen felt complete freedom to hold himself accountable in the areas of faithfulness to God as well as faithfulness in thoughts, words, and deeds by confessing his "many ups and downs in the struggle to remain anchored in Jesus" (RD:210–211). It was through this exercise in honesty and openness that Nouwen felt even more connected with Ball in a deeper way that nurtured in him greater faithfulness and prayerfulness.

Their friendship, however, like any other, was not exempt from being tested. Fourteen months after coming to L'Arche, what had begun as a beautiful friendship suddenly broke as a result of Nouwen's clingy dependency. Their treasured friendship was restored eventually. In fact it deepened so considerably that years after this test, Nouwen could say with confidence, "Today we are committed friends, as people of faith, as co-leaders of Daybreak, and as men committed to share with and support each other" (SJ:135). Not only was their relationship a demonstration of mutual sharing at the soul level, but it was clearly an experience of "a unity of souls that gives nobility and sincerity to love," as Nouwen describes the gift of friendship (BJ:Jan 7). As well, both Nouwen and Ball exhibited mutual alignment and conformity of lives through their shared commitment to minister to and serve the people with disabilities at L'Arche community. Both of them embraced the same mission to work with the marginalized.

Mutuality with Sue Mosteller

Nouwen's relationships with Nathan Ball and Sue Mosteller formed a sort of "trinity" of friendship. Nouwen and Mosteller first met in 1981, but their formal connection began five years later, after Nouwen accepted the call to be Daybreak's resident pastor. With a common interest in spirituality, they started working closely together as co-pastors in the Dayspring House of Prayer at L'Arche.

In a personal interview, Mosteller recalled a particularly difficult period in her life when she nearly burned out and could hardly operate in her ministry at L'Arche. Nouwen was there for her, encouraging her to take some time off to sort things out. He helped her go beyond her feelings of being stuck, always gently pushing her to take risks. When Nouwen suffered a mental breakdown, it became Mosteller's turn to provide him with much-needed support. Nouwen recounts vividly how God used Mosteller in his life amid his depression to radically alter his perspective about his new calling. In one of her visits, Mosteller's words proved to be healing for Nouwen, helping him to slowly recover and gain a renewed sense of vocation. Mosteller said, "Henri, you're always talking about yourself being the prodigal son, and you're often talking about yourself being the elder son, but now it's time for you to become the father! That's who you're called to be" (HT:130–131). The relationship between Nouwen and Mosteller proved to be a mutually encouraging one for each of their spiritual journeys. What they were privileged to enjoy together, along with Ball, was a purifying communal friendship.

Mutuality with Robert Jonas

Another close friend in Henri Nouwen's circle, with whom he shared many moments of mutual vulnerability and trust, was Robert Jonas, or Jonas, as Nouwen would fondly address him. They had their first encounter at Harvard University in 1983, when Jonas was finishing his doctoral studies there. Jonas was mesmerized the first time he heard Nouwen lecture with great passion and conviction about Jesus. Though the relationship started with Jonas asking Nouwen to be his spiritual director, the two eventually ended up as peers who committed themselves to accompanying each other on their respective journeys through both good and challenging times.

Despite some struggles and misunderstandings in their long-standing friendship, Nouwen learned through Jonas some of the greatest principles on the sacred nature of friendship. For example, he realized the vital role of distance in living out real friendship—that "in a true friendship, two people make a dance" (RD:65). Likewise, he learned that friendship demands mutual forgiveness, "a constant willingness to forgive each other for not being Christ" (*RD*:65). Most of all, Nouwen discovered the hard way that "friendship requires closeness, affection, support, and mutual encouragement, but also distance, space to grow, freedom to be different, and solitude" (*RD*:65).

In the relationships Henri Nouwen enjoyed with Ball, Mosteller, and Jonas, among others, mutuality and complementarity were evident dynamics that made their intimate connections work. Together they possessed a common heart beating for each other, for God, and for the community to which they belonged.

For Further Focused Reading

Compassion: A Reflection on the Christian Life

In Memoriam

In the Name of Jesus: Reflections on Christian Leadership

Living It Out

1. Engage in a brief *lectio divina* exercise using any of the "one-anothering" passages mentioned in this chapter: Romans 15:7, 1 Thessalonians 5:11, or Galatians 6:2. Prayerfully discern how you might live out the biblical admonition of personally ministering to someone in your community in a mutually beneficial way that allows for the natural experience of complementarity.

2. Think of how you might practice the dynamic of confession and forgiveness within your small group at church or any group in which you are regularly involved. Single out a person you might open up to in a transparent way about a burden you carry, and confess your true fears, doubts, and struggles. Allow yourself to be healed by this simple process. Or ask God if you need to seek out someone's forgiveness, and go to that person in boldness and humility. Leave the results to God.

3. This week, look for opportunities to receive anything from someone with gladness of heart. At the same time, look for chances to thoughtfully give something to somebody. Whether you end up giving or receiving—or both—just be grateful for the gift God may choose to open up for you.

Prayer of the Heart

Ever-loving Father, Son, and Holy Spirit,

The more I find my sisters, brothers, and myself in you, the more you teach me both to give and to receive generously. Show me what is at the root of my unloving habits of critiquing people before I know them, of attempting to put myself above them in some way. Replace that in me with your way of selflessly being the one to wash others' feet as well as wholeheartedly receiving the gifts of others. Free me from my need so that I no longer seek to find ways to defend myself against the needs of others. Show me someone you have put into my life as a gift whom I have failed to value, and may we be gracious to one another as we walk further together on this road toward fullness of life in you.

Amen.

SIX

Solidarity

A Connected Heart

"We are not alone; beyond the differences
that separate us, we share one common
humanity and thus belong to each other."
—*Our Greatest Gift*

Henri Nouwen often uses the word "solidarity" in relation to community life, although by no means does he limit his use of the word to this. For instance, he refers to solidarity in conjunction with God's relationship with us as well as our relationship with humankind as a whole: "[Jesus] broke down the pyramidal structures of relationship between God and people as well as those among people and offered a new model: the circle, where God lives in full solidarity with the people and the people with one another" (*IVL*:41).

In typical Nouwen usage, solidarity means closely identifying with and connecting with others. Whereas in general we are prone to elevate the notion of differences, Nouwen accentuates sameness and commonality. Inclusion, not exclusion, is uppermost in his thinking. His focus is on the existential reality of our common sense of belonging. For Nouwen, everyone and everything belongs together within a unified field.

Such a dynamic concept of connectedness—applied to God, to people, to ministry—is key to Nouwen's spirituality. We see God's solidarity with humankind manifested openly when God takes the form of a man in the person of Christ to be just like us. "The joy of belonging to the human race," Nouwen says, is also "the joy of Jesus, who is Emmanuel: God-with-us" (*BJ*:Jan 31). A fuller understanding of God's solidarity reveals that God is not just with us, but "he suffers with us" (*RP*:194). Nouwen wants us to realize the connectedness of God's story with our own story. We need to see that "we are an ongoing revelation of God," and therefore we can "claim our own suffering and joy as part of God's" (*RP*:193). Making these vital connections is what brings about compassion in us.

There is also a sense in which our solidarity with God through the compassionate Christ is shown in our attempt to live our lives for others (*LM*:34). Finally, we keep in mind that all of us are in solidarity with each other as a community of God as well as a human family created by the same God who is the Creator of all. In short, before God we are one, and nothing can alter that reality.

> "Communion with God and solidarity with all of humanity always go together."
>
> —*Beloved*

These various facets of solidarity necessarily intertwine. "You cannot live in communion with God without living in solidarity with people; it is essentially the same," Nouwen asserts (*B*:23). In Nouwen's characteristic cross illustration, this is like the vertical beam, representing our relationship with God, crossing the horizontal beam, representing our relationship with one another. Inevitably our relationship with God impacts our relationship with people, as 1 John 1:7 makes clear: "But if we walk in the light as he himself is in the light, we have fellowship with one another."

Solidarity with Humankind and Our Community

The weight Henri Nouwen places on our universal identification with each other—whether it be with the entire human race or our particular communities—is huge. He references our shared humanity quite often and elevates our commonality. Our oneness as a people gives us more than enough reason to celebrate. Nouwen identifies with this exultant feeling. Recalling the joy he experienced while walking with thousands of others in Alabama from Selma to Montgomery during the historic civil rights march, Nouwen remarks, "All I felt was a deep sameness, a profound communion with all people, an exhilarating sense of brotherhood and sisterhood ... the joy of being the same as others, of belonging to one human family" (*GG*:26). We really can find a "joyful solidarity with humanity," since we are all participants in the human struggle (*RP*:194). The sentiment Nouwen displays speaks volumes about his own inner longing to connect deeply with people and his hunger for the experience of community in whatever form it takes. He is deeply committed to bridging the gap between people because he firmly believes that "we are children of the same God and members of the same human family" (*BJ*:July 22).

In much the same way—perhaps in a more intimate fashion—we are in solidarity with one another as an assembled community. Nouwen thus proudly proclaims:

> This ... is the mystery of our new way of being together. It has become possible to be together in compassion because we have been given a share in God's compassion. In and through this compassion, we can begin to live in solidarity with each other as fully and intimately as God lives with us. (*C*:22)

The spirit of compassion residing in us is what strengthens our inner resolve to conduct our lives in a manner true to our call to solidarity. To Nouwen, it seems inconceivable to operate as a community—particularly as a gathered Christian community—apart from this posture of solidarity.

Solidarity in Weakness

Nowhere is our experience of solidarity felt more deeply than through an open acknowledgment of our fragility as mortal human beings. Community is developed in a more profound way when we learn to come together in our poverty instead of our wealth, health, and strength (*BJ*:Mar 18). As Nouwen puts it, "As a community of faith we remind one another constantly that we form a fellowship of the weak, transparent to him who speaks to us in our lonely places of existence" (*OS*:24). In our state of weakness we find solace and strength in each other's presence. Nouwen views an explicitly Christian community of faith as ideally "a faithful fellowship of the weak in which, through a repeated confession and forgiveness of sins, the strength of Jesus Christ is revealed and celebrated" (PW:101).

Henri Nouwen's decadelong immersion in the L'Arche Daybreak community stands as a testimony to his genuine desire to be in solidarity with weak and broken people. "Daybreak is not a place of power" but a place of the poor (RD:192). He deeply believed that "the poor of spirit are "given to us for our conversion" (RP:155). "In choosing to become poor with the poor at L'Arche," Nouwen underwent massive transformational shifts in his conviction and perspective (RD:154). For one, through his desire to belong with people, with disabilities considered by many to be on the margins of society, Nouwen experienced a radical self-confrontation in which he was able to face his own handicaps, thus paving a much deeper way to identify with the true fellowship of the weak (see RD:220).

It makes sense that as we recognize our commonality as human beings, "we can participate in the care of God who came, not to be powerful but powerless, not to be different but the same, not to take our pain away but to share it" (OS:43). Through such participation our hearts open all the more widely for the sake of one another, leading to a much stronger formation of community. There is, in fact, tremendous healing power in our experience of human solidarity because in our fragile existence, "we can taste the joy of being human and foretaste our communion with all people" (GG:32).

> "The heart of God, the heart of all creation, and our own hearts become one in love."
>
> —Bread for the Journey

Our solidarity extends to death itself; even in this we are able to affirm that indeed we are all the same, "feeling our equality as a grace" (IM:44). As we all "partake of this world's inevitable transitions," Nouwen admonishes us to "face not only our own deaths, then, but willingly allow for the deaths of those we know and love and live with" (TMD:104–105). For in death, which is an intimate part of our humanity, we embrace our ultimate experience of solidarity with every soul on earth.

For Further Focused Reading

Compassion: A Reflection on the Christian Life

In Memoriam

The Road to Peace

Living It Out

1. Ponder this question: What can I do as a first step to feel connected with people considered to be on the margins of society? Search online for a local branch of L'Arche or a similar community, like a nearby homeless shelter; schedule a visit, and enter that world with an open spirit. Pray for wisdom as to how you might identify with the members of the community in some shape or form.

2. In your daily examen, reflect on and name your own poverty, your own handicap, your own limitations. Identify a group with which you can be in solidarity and experience yourself being immersed in the "fellowship of the weak," where you can also celebrate with gratitude the freeing reality that all is grace.

3. Contemplate the current reality of your own community, and ask the Spirit to reveal to you how you can actively rally behind a common cause, an issue, or any pressing concern for which you can offer your all-out support. Think of some other practical ways in which you can visibly demonstrate your solidarity with your community. Be willing to take some risks and baby steps to get something rolling by faith.

Prayer of the Heart

O God our life,

You made us in your own image and yet somehow also took on our flesh.

At our creation, you breathed your life into us as pure gift, and every person we have ever encountered has that touch that could only come from your hand. As I unpack my own life hidden in Christ and find you indwelling me, where the life that you live and the life you have given me are ever more the same, help me to see you indwelling the people I will pass today—whether strangers on the street or my closest loved ones in my own home. As grateful as I am that you are here with me, I am even more awestruck that you are here with us. Because of that, may I never again see another person as a stranger, but may I behold you, who indwell me, in them.

Amen.

Part III

Commission
A Life Given

"The Spirit of Christ sends us into the world. To
the degree that we are guided not by our fears but
by the power of the Spirit, we become aware of the
needs of the world and we experience a deep desire
to be of service."

—*A Cry for Mercy*

"[Ministry] is at the core of the Christian life.
No Christian is a Christian without being a
minister.... Whatever form the Christian ministry
takes, the basis is always the same: to lay down one's
life for one's friends."

—*Creative Ministry*

"As the Beloved ones, our greatest fulfillment lies
in becoming bread for the world. That is the most
intimate expression of our deepest desire to give
ourselves to each other."

—*Life of the Beloved*

"He went down with them and stood on a level place. A large crowd of his disciples was there and a great number of people from all over ... who had come to hear him and to be healed of their diseases."

—Luke 6:17–18 NIV

We now catch the full picture of the threefold spiritual movement portrayed in Luke 6:12–19. First, we see Jesus spend time in communion with his Father. Then he forms a community composed of twelve men whom he entrusts with a specific commission. This progression—communion, community, commission—directly corresponds to the symbolic journey from solitude to community to ministry that Henri Nouwen references consistently in his writings about the flow of the spiritual life.

The final movement that completes our trilogy—our commission to ministry—is highlighted in Mark's Gospel with utmost clarity: "He went up the mountain and called to him those whom he wanted, and they came to him. And he appointed twelve, whom he also named apostles, to be with him, and to be sent out to proclaim the message" (Mark 3:13–14). The pattern is evident: We set apart time to commune with God in solitude, then establish a community with whom we share our life together and give our lives to others in response to God's commission for us to do ministry. This corresponds to Henri Nouwen's schema: "Communion not only creates community, but community always leads to mission" (BH:76).

God's commission for us to engage actively in ministry to the world is never to be viewed apart from God's interior work in us as God's beloved. Henri Nouwen well understands the priority of *being* over *doing*—the outward movement naturally flows from the inward. The reality is that "we are called to connect, not so much by what we do, but by who we

> "Communion not only creates community, but community always leads to mission."
>
> *—With Burning Hearts*

are" (*LR*:30). Our claimed identity is what leads to our proclaimed ministry. Nouwen underscores the necessary connection between these two: "Ministry is the manifestation in our own person of the presence of Christ in the world. The more fully we have imagined who we truly are and the more our true identity becomes visible, the more we become living witnesses of Jesus Christ" (*G!*:31). He reminds us:

> When our ministry does not emerge from a personal encounter, it quickly becomes a tiring routine and a boring job. On the other hand, when our spiritual life no longer leads to an active ministry, it quickly degenerates into introspection and self-scrutiny, and thus loses its dynamism. Our life in Christ and our ministry in his name belong together as the two beams of the cross. (*SWC*:16)

The truth, as Nouwen sees it, is that "it is in the silence and solitude of prayer that the minister becomes minister" (*LR*:51). Ministry is simply the natural outflow of our vibrant relationship and deep connectedness with the Source of our spiritual life.

"Wasting time with God is an act of ministry."
—*The Living Reminder*

Henri Nouwen carefully points out that our ministry endeavor ought not to be dependent on our well-formed and informed opinions concerning the relevant issues of our time. Rather we should locate its foundation in "the permanent, intimate relationship with the incarnate Word, Jesus" and draw from there "words, advice, and guidance" (*INJ*:31). As a Christian leader and minister, Nouwen is fully convinced that

> when we are securely rooted in personal intimacy with the source of life, it will be possible to remain flexible without being relativistic, convinced without being rigid, willing to confront without being offensive, gentle and forgiving without being soft, and true witnesses without being manipulative. (*INJ*:32)

Our intimate communion with God defines the character and quality of our ministry. It is our tight connectedness to the Source that both yields and sustains our entire ministry undertaking.

Christ himself exemplified this truth for us through his abiding relationship with his Father. Nouwen elucidates:

All through his life Jesus considers his relationship with the Father as the center, beginning, and the end of his ministry.... It is obvious that Jesus does not maintain his relationship with the Father as a means of fulfilling his ministry. On the contrary, his relationship with the Father is the core of his ministry. (*LR*:50–51)

Here again, spirituality and ministry cannot be separated from each other, just as, for Nouwen, prayer and service, contemplation and action, the mystical and the prophetic, always go hand in hand.

In the high priestly prayer recorded in John's Gospel, Jesus prays to his Father for his community of followers shortly before his impending death: "As you sent me into the world, I have sent them into the world" (John 17:18). In accordance with the Great Commission (Matthew 28:19–20), we, as the Church, whom Nouwen refers to as "Christ living in the world," are mandated by no less than Jesus himself to go into the world and make disciples of all nations. This, according to Nouwen, is the true mission of the Church as a community of faith. More than just supporting, nurturing, and guiding its own members, we are called "to be a witness to the love of God made visible in Jesus" to the world (*BJ*:Nov 5). In one of the diary entries in *Sabbatical Journey*, Henri Nouwen articulates his unswerving commitment to spread the good news of Jesus to all people:

> "Part of the essence of being the Church is being 'a living witness for Christ in the world.'"
>
> —*Bread for the Journey*

I feel deeply called to witness for Jesus as the one who is the source of my own spiritual journey and thus create the possibility for other people to know Jesus and commit themselves to him. I am so truly convinced that the Spirit of God is present in our midst and that each person can be touched by God's Spirit in ways far beyond my own comprehension and intention. (*SJ*:51)

In Nouwen's mind, there is hardly any question about the primacy of announcing the gospel and speaking about Jesus and his work of salvation. "What we have received is so beautiful and so rich that we cannot hold it for ourselves but feel compelled to bring it to every human being we meet," Nouwen says with conviction (*BJ*:Aug 5–6). Yet, at the same time, our commission to ministry is even more expansive, encompassing the tasks of healing and reconciliation as well.

Healing and Reconciliation

A critical part of the mandate entrusted to us by God involves participating in the ministry of healing and reconciliation. In a broken and hurting world desperate for "healing, forgiveness, reconciliation, and most of all unconditional love" we cannot—we dare not—ignore the seriousness of this task. As we seek to attend to it, we do so in the power of the name of Jesus, outside of which our ministry will be rendered completely impotent (*BJ*:Nov 6). To the Christ-centered Nouwen, all ministry is about unapologetically "acting in the name of Jesus" (*BJ*: Nov 18).

The Task of Healing

It is easy to think that ministry is mere performance, when in reality it is something that demands trust on our part. For instance, "We have to trust that if we are the son or daughter of God, power will go out from us and people will be healed" (*SL*:44), not because of us but because of the One in whose name and power we put our trust. Healing takes place not because we possess healing powers ourselves. True ministry—healing ministry included—happens "when we bring others in touch with more than we ourselves are—the center of being, the reality of the unseen—the Father who is the source of life and healing" (*TMD*:75). God is the true healer, not us. But although we are not the source of healing, we remain vital instruments for the physical or spiritual healing of others.

The Work of Gratitude and Compassion

The ministry of healing can be demonstrated via two avenues: gratitude and compassion. Healing usually takes place when people are ushered into a position of gratitude. Gratitude in general means "to live life as a gift to be received gratefully." But, as Nouwen emphasizes, gratitude as the gospel speaks about it "embraces *all* of life: the good and the bad, the joyful and painful, the holy and the not so holy" (*SL*:47). As I previously mentioned, the word "Eucharist" literally means "thanksgiving." Thus, to live a eucharistic life, "gratitude needs to be discovered and to be lived with great inner attentiveness" (*BH*:93). There is tremendous inner healing that can be experienced when people learn to live in this manner.

Likewise there is healing in compassionate caring. Compassionate ministry involves entering into the sobering reality of human pain. That is what true compassion means—"to suffer with, to live with those who suffer" (SL:49). It has to do with "full immersion in the condition of being human" (C:4). Healing happens when someone dares to enter into our pain and suffering with a real heart of compassion. The Gospels portray Jesus as a compassionate healer of the blind, the lame, the sick, the demon-possessed, and burdened sinners in general.

Wounded Healers

We are all broken, wounded people in deep need of spiritual healing. But the challenging question that Henri Nouwen poses to each of us is, how can we put our woundedness in the service of others? He says, "When our wounds cease to be a source of shame and become a source of healing, we have become wounded healers" (BJ:July 8). A wounded healer is one who can attentively listen to a wounded person without the compelling need to share about his own woundedness unless called for. Nouwen warns about a form of "spiritual exhibitionism" that is unhelpful and only serves to make ourselves the focal point. As Nouwen assures us, "We have to trust that our own bandaged wounds will allow us to listen to others with our whole being. That is healing" (BJ:July 10).

> "A eucharistic life is one lived in gratitude."
>
> —With Burning Hearts

At the same time, a profound understanding of our own pain is what enables us to convert our weakness into strength and offer our experience appropriately as a source of healing for others. For "once the pain is accepted and understood," Nouwen reasons, "a denial is no longer necessary, and ministry can become a healing service" (WH:87). We are truly wounded but genuinely healers just the same.

The Task of Reconciliation

Henri Nouwen asks and answers for us three basic questions pertaining to the ministry of reconciliation and our commission from God: What is our task? Why is it our task? How do we carry out this task?

First, Nouwen is ever mindful of the fact that the sacred task of reconciliation is to reveal the truth that "all people belong together as members of one family under God" and also to incorporate this truth into the reality of everyday life (BJ:Dec 25). Why? Because God sent Jesus to reconcile us with God, and as reconciled people, we have been entrusted with the ministry of reconciliation (see 2 Corinthians 5:18).

So how do we begin this task of reconciliation? "First and foremost by claiming for ourselves that God through Christ has reconciled us to God"—that is, "that we are forgiven, that we have received new hearts, new spirits, new eyes to see, and new ears to hear" (BJ:Dec 26). Nouwen maintains that as we realize the extent to which we ourselves have been reconciled with God, we can then be ambassadors of reconciliation for other people. We will do all we can to facilitate people's reconciliation with God and with other human beings, for we are all meant to experience the reality of that to which we are called by God. It touches us at our very core, "in the most hidden parts of our souls," which is why "God gave reconciliation to us as a ministry that never ends" (BJ:Dec 27, 29). Such is a definitive part of our mission, of our being sent into the world by God in the same way that Jesus was. As we live our lives "as missions" and embrace the conviction of being sent, we are bound to recognize even more specifically what we were sent to accomplish, and come to the full realization that "the years of our lives are years 'on a mission'" (BJ:Apr 23–24).

Commission and Prayer

We have already seen how the experiential realities of both communion and community are contained within the dynamic of prayer. And by prayer we mean the very breath of our spiritual life, as Nouwen regards it, prayer "in the sense of a prayerful life, a life lived in connection with Christ" (LR:34). The same holds true for commission and prayer because for Nouwen ministry and spirituality are virtually indivisible. We might even say the Great Commission and the Great Commandment are twin mandates that deserve our equal attention.

Nouwen clearly embodies a nondualistic mind-set (a both-and versus an either-or mentality) when it comes to the intertwining spiritual realities he endorses, such as loving God and loving others; prayer and service;

contemplation and action; the mystical and the prophetic. Here is how he elaborates on the inseparable link between ministry and spirituality:

> Just as all Jesus' words and actions emerge from his communion with his Father, so all our words and actions must emerge from our communion with Jesus. "In all truth I tell you," he says, "whoever believes in me will perform even greater works.... Whatever you ask for in my name I will do" (John 14:12–13). It is this profound truth that reveals the relationship between the spiritual life and the life of ministry. (*BJ*:Nov 17)

Nouwen reinforces this by stating that "when we live in communion with God's Spirit, we can only be witnesses, because wherever we go and whomever we meet, God's Spirit will manifest itself through us." Indeed in our spiritual life, our spirit and God's Spirit always bear joint witness (*BJ*:June 18).

Just as communion and commission are entwined, "prayer cannot be considered external to the process of ministry," Nouwen stresses. "Prayer is the way to both the heart of God and the heart of the world." It is about "living in unceasing communion with God and God's people and thus seeing and proclaiming the rightful order of things, the divine order" (*LFL*:100, 102). Thus, "service and prayer cannot be separated; they are related to each other as the Yin and Yang of the Japanese Circle" (*LR*:12–13). Prayer is service and service is prayer. Nouwen explains their intimate and interactive dynamics:

> "Once the pain is accepted and understood, a denial is no longer necessary, and ministry can become a healing service."
> —*The Wounded Healer*

> If prayer leads us into a deeper unity with the compassionate Christ, it will always give rise to concrete acts of service. And if concrete acts of service do indeed lead us to a deeper solidarity with the poor, the hungry, the sick, the dying, and the oppressed, they will always give rise to prayer. In prayer we meet Christ, and in him all human suffering. In service we meet people, and in them the suffering Christ. (*C*:117)

Here we see that "prayer is the way to both the heart of God and the heart of the world—precisely because they have been joined through the suffering of Jesus Christ" (*LFL*:100). Once again using his favorite metaphor, Nouwen says, "Prayer is to go to the hub. That's solitude, that's the heart. Prayer is going to your heart, but it's also going to the heart of the world and the spokes get together right there" (*B*:23). This again shows how communion and commission most naturally intersect.

The three chapters that follow deal with Christ's commission, which, in Nouwen's vocabulary, pertains to the synonymous concepts of mission and ministry. We focus here on the key constructs of service, compassion, and hospitality. Correspondingly, our attention revolves around what it means to minister in a selfless, caring, and spacious manner—inner dispositions of the heart that Henri Nouwen embodied in his own ministry.

Personal Ponderings

1. Under the general umbrella of God's universal commission, do I personally sense a specific ministry call from God? If so, how do I envision such call? In what ways do I see myself uniquely fulfilling it? What impact do I think I would have in the world as a result of my response to God's call for me?

2. When I reflect on the idea of giving my life over to do ministry, exactly what do I understand that to mean? What might be involved in being willing to lay down my life for the benefit of others? If it is true, as Nouwen insists, that every Christian is a minister, how do I see myself as a minister?

3. One of the Christian buzzwords of our day is the term "missional." What does this concept mean to me? Do I have a clear grasp of God's mission and/or the mission of the Church as the "sent out" community? When I entertain the notion of mission in relation to God's mandate (or commission), what does that encompass or entail? What is being required of me as the "commissioned one"?

SEVEN

Service

A Selfless Heart

"True ministry goes far beyond the giving
of gifts. It requires giving of self."
—*¡Gracias!*

Henri Nouwen often uses the term "service" interchangeably with both "mission" and "ministry." He reckons all three as the overflow of our love for God and for our fellow human beings because, as he contends, "if you are living in communion with God, if you know you are the Beloved, and if you make yourself available for service, you cannot do other than minister" (SD:131). In a more definitive fashion, service represents the true praxis of ministry, meaning it is ministry concretely lived out or put into specific action. The emphasis lies on the thrust of serving or giving something out or away. Put simply, to truly minister is to humbly serve. And such humble service requires a selfless, self-giving heart, a posture Nouwen modeled compellingly for us in a variety of ways and contexts. He served God sacrificially, and he gave of himself to others willingly and unreservedly out of the abundance of his heart. He was a true servant of God.

For Nouwen, serving God and serving others are mutually inclusive. Service runs vertically and horizontally—both to Christ and to others— in a simultaneous course. When we serve others, we are in actuality serving Christ; as we serve Christ, we do so through serving others (see Matthew 25:35–40). This is why he could claim "service to the neighbor is also service to God" (LR:32). Even when it comes to the Great Commandment—loving God, loving neighbor—Nouwen underlines his conviction that the first and second commandments are equal and inseparable: "The first commandment receives concreteness and specificity through the second; the second commandment becomes possible through the first" (LR:32).

Nouwen cautions us about the predictable consequences when we fail to maintain integration between the first and second commandments:

> Service outside of God becomes self-seeking, and self-seeking service leads to manipulation, and manipulation to power games, and power games to violence, and violence to destruction—even when it falls under the name of ministry.... The true challenge is to make service to our neighbor the manifestation and celebration of our total and undivided service to God. Only when all of our service finds its source and goal in God can we be free from the desire for power and proceed to serve our neighbors for their sake and not for our own. (SWC:64–65)

Real service draws its energy and strength from God, the Source—without whom we can do nothing—and attributes its outcome to the same Source, who alone deserves credit.

The Call to Self-Giving

In one of his heartfelt prayers to Jesus, Nouwen recounts what a life of service to God assumes: "It is a life of intimate communion with you.... But it is also a life that calls me to give all that I am in the service of your love for the world" (HSH:43). For Nouwen, giving all means literally giving all of himself, including his very life. Nouwen feels certain that "giving away our lives for others is the greatest of all human acts" (BJ:Apr 30). In fact, according to him, "the beginning and the end of all Christian leadership"—and all of ministry, for that matter—"is to give your life for others" (WH:72).

"Service outside of God becomes self-seeking."

—The Selfless Way of Christ

Such a position is consistent with what Nouwen perceives genuine gospel living to be. With a good dose of realism, he poignantly notes, "Life is a long journey of preparation—of preparing oneself to truly die for others. It is a series of deaths in which we are asked to release many forms of clinging and to move increasingly from needing others to living for them" (*BM*:65).

What might he mean by this challenge to lay down our lives for others—particularly for our friends (*CM*:114)? Not surprisingly this could refer to our willingness to literally die for others. But Nouwen also means "making our own lives—our sorrows and joys, our despair and hope, our loneliness and experience of intimacy—available to others as sources of new life" (*BJ*:Apr 14). Giving of ourselves and our lives in this way—including sharing our life struggles—is in itself a form of service, since our openness about our own life can lend courage and hope to others. In conjunction with our ministry, it is valuable to ask ourselves, "'Is my sharing of my struggle in the service of the one who seeks my help?'" (*IVL*:72–73). If our answer is in the affirmative, then our struggle becomes a worthy gift to give away to others.

> "One of the greatest gifts we can give others is ourselves."
>
> —*Bread for the Journey*

To the question of why one has to be willing to lay down one's life for others, there really is only one answer, according to Nouwen: to give new life. After all, "all functions of ministry are life-giving" with the aim "to open new perspectives, to offer new insight, to give new strength, to break through the chains of death and destruction, and to create new life which can be affirmed" (*CM*:115). For Nouwen, "Christian leadership is called ministry precisely to express that in the service of others new life can be brought about" (*WH*:75).

Henri Nouwen is well aware that the sacred call to self-giving is utterly meaningless if we do not have a self worth giving away. In the same vein, it does not make sense to lay down a life we do not have; none of us can give away anything we do not first possess (*IVL*:65). This sheds light on why, for Nouwen, both self-affirmation and self-denial constitute the identity of the minister. As he explains, "Self-affirmation and self-emptying are not opposites because no man can give

> "All functions of ministry are life-giving."
>
> —*Creative Ministry*

away what he does not have. No one can give himself in love when he is not aware of himself. Nobody can come to intimacy without having found his identity" (CM:51–52). When we are secure in the fact that God loves us unconditionally, we are able to freely love others. Nouwen says that this means "trusting that you do not need to protect your own security but can give yourself completely to the service of others." He hastens to add, "You cannot give yourself to others if you do not own yourself, and you can only truly own yourself when you have been fully received in unconditional love" (IVL:65–66).

No less than Jesus, the Son of God, illustrated this through the extraordinary example of his own earthly life:

> Jesus lived thirty years in a simple family. There he became a man who knew who he was and where he wanted to go. Only then was he ready to empty himself and give his life for others. That is the way of all ministry. (CM:52)

The Experience of Downward Mobility

If it is true—as Nouwen would have us all affirm—that "to live a spiritual life means to become living Christs," then it follows that we are to pattern our lives according to the way of Christ. To be sure, "the way of Christ is a self-emptying way" (G!:116). Doubtless it is a selfless way leading to the countercultural experience of what Nouwen describes as "downward mobility" (SWC:20). Out of this reality, Nouwen developed his own theology of weakness and powerlessness, which formed and informed the main trajectory of his ministry.

Nouwen relentlessly emphasizes that downward mobility requires aggressively saying no to what he reckons as "the three compulsions of the world: ... the desire to be relevant, the desire for popularity, and the desire for power" (WOH:25)—the same temptations Jesus himself confronted and to which we as ministers get subjected time and again. Downward mobility requires making a radical shift "from a concern for relevance to a life of prayer, from worries about popularity to communal and mutual ministry, and from a leadership built on power to a leadership

"You cannot give yourself to others if you do not own yourself."

—The Inner Voice of Love

in which we critically discern where God is leading us and our people" (*INJ*:71–72). What could be more counterintuitive and countercultural than this?

Henri Nouwen, of course, did not just talk about downward mobility; he himself lived it out by choosing to spend the last decade of his life serving the disabled people at L'Arche Daybreak in Ontario. Leaving the Ivy League world of Harvard University for an obscure community of folks with all types of disabilities was a major step downward for Nouwen. But in his heart he genuinely wanted to belong with those who did not "belong" in society—at least from the narrow standpoint of some people. Nouwen had the firsthand privilege of taking care of Adam, one of the most severely disabled young men in the community, who in turn offered him "a sense of belonging" (*A*:26), rooted him in the truth of his own physical being, anchored him in his chosen community, and provided him a profound sense of the presence of God in their life together. In serving Adam, Nouwen experienced deep healing for himself and was led to a clearer understanding of the

> "The way of Christ is a self-emptying way."
> —¡*Gracias!*

true meaning of poverty as well as the mysterious grace of the love of God at work (*A*:back flap). There at L'Arche Daybreak, Nouwen gave of himself selflessly, serving a community he learned to embrace wholeheartedly as his very own.

Prophetic Service

Sacrificial service, as Nouwen's own life bore out, includes several facets beyond our pastoral and priestly ministerial roles. It is by no means complete unless it extends to the prophetic dimension, involving the call to guide others into the vision of the future. Prophets, says Nouwen, can speak only "from the vision which guides their own lives day and night." He continues, "It is in the encounter with the prophetic minister that strength is found to break out of myopic viewpoints and courage is given to move beyond safe and secure boundaries" (*LR*:67). Nouwen was careful to warn, "A prophetic ministry which guides toward a new future requires hard, painful unmasking of our illusions" (*LR*:63).

Henri Nouwen was and continues to be a prophet of our time. He maintains that "our service to others will include our helping them see the glory breaking through—not only where they are active but also where they are being acted upon" (FWH:119). It is about waiting for change to happen, not just inner change of heart but societal change. Nouwen believes that we all are prophetic agents of social change. To him it is undeniable that "changing the human heart and changing human society are not separate tasks, but are as interconnected as the two beams of the cross" (WH:20).

Henri Nouwen's spirituality is not merely an interior matter but something that has profound implications in terms of his relationship with others and the world in general. He holds to the conviction that "the love of God lived in its fullest sense leads to a most selfless dedication to the neighbor" and that our most "intimate union with God leads to the most creative involvement in the contemporary world" (GD:177). The contemplative life, for Nouwen, is never removed from action; it is a life of vision—seeing reality and the world transparently—carried out through our ministry (see SF:5).

"Intimate union with God leads to the most creative involvement in the contemporary world."

—The Genesee Diary

Wherever we turn, we witness suffering of all kinds, of individuals as well as communities—persecution, abuse, mistreatment, victimization from senseless crimes. We cannot help but ask how in the world we can direct people to "shalom," a state of "well-being of mind, heart, and body, individually and communally" (BJ:May 30). Nouwen himself asks us this arresting question: "Are we willing to give our lives in the service of peace?" (BJ:May 30). In his heart, Nouwen is convinced that "as we call one another to respond to the cries of [the] people and work together for justice and peace, we are caring for Christ, who suffered and died for the salvation of our world" (BJ:July 19).

For Further Focused Reading

Creative Ministry

The Inner Voice of Love: A Journey Through Anguish to Freedom

The Selfless Way of Christ: Downward Mobility and the Spiritual Life

Living It Out

1. Do a brief *lectio divina* on Philippians 2:1–11. Resolve to "lay down your life for a friend" by openly sharing your most difficult struggle lately as a true act of service to your friend, in hope that this will be received as a precious gift coming from your heart. Pray for a sincere effort at reaching out with utmost sensitivity.

2. Explore possibilities for a meaningful and concrete engagement with social justice and/or peace concerns locally. Ask yourself how you can make even a small change in your own world. What sacrifice are you willing to make? What can you personally give up to make something happen?

3. As you reflect on the challenge of pursuing downward mobility in your current life situation, identify some concrete steps you can take to simplify your life and start acting on them accordingly. Perhaps deliberately cutting out some of your high-profile activities in favor of quiet service to the poor and underprivileged, away from the limelight and the applause of others? What are some other self-emptying acts you can do that would prove to be life-giving for others? Journal about your thoughts.

Prayer of the Heart

Crucified and Risen Lord,

You set us an example, teaching us to do as you did: seeking not to be served but to serve, and to live no longer for ourselves but for love of you and those around us. Teach me to live fully in you so that I can have real life to give generously to others. Help me to lay down my illusions of protecting myself as I learn to walk in the way of your cross and find that your life grows in me as I seek your death and resurrection rather than my own preservation. Give me, today, someone to serve in this love that you have poured into my heart.

Amen.

EIGHT

Compassion

A Caring Heart

"Out of his solitude Jesus reached out his caring
hand to the people in need. In the lonely place
his care grew strong and mature. And from there
he entered into a healing closeness with his fellow
human beings."

—*Out of Solitude*

Henri Nouwen stands on his staunch belief that the call to compassionate living is central to the Christian life. More pointedly, it is the
driving force for our relational ministry toward others. Derived from the
radical nature of Christ's own command in Luke 6:36 ("Be compassionate just as your Father is compassionate" NJB), the call mirrors the very
character of God as compassionate, the God who expects us to live our
lives compassionately through prayer and action (*C*:8). Nouwen presents
compassion as a reality "where ministry and spirituality touch each other.
It ... is the fruit of solitude and the basis for all ministry" (*WOH*:33). The
fact of the matter is, "in and through solitude we do not move away from
people. On the contrary, we move closer to them through compassionate
ministry" (*WOH*:39). Our inward experience with God is what propels
our outward action toward others. The God of compassion with whom we
commune is the One who moves our hearts to feel compassion for others.

What makes compassion inherently difficult is the fact that "it requires the inner disposition to go with others to the place where they are weak, vulnerable, lonely, and broken.... Yet perhaps our greatest gift is our ability to enter into solidarity with those who suffer" (*SC*:19). When the challenge of compassion is taken up seriously, our whole outlook can radically shift. In Henri Nouwen's more optimistic perspective, "compassion makes us see beauty in the midst of misery, hope in the center of pain" (*AG*:113). Such a promising view of compassion is only possible when it is founded upon and bathed in prayer. That is what internally drives us to freely live a compassionate lifestyle, Nouwen assures us, "even when it does not evoke a grateful response or bring immediate rewards" (*OH*:96).

> "Compassion grows with the inner recognition that your neighbor shares your humanity with you."
>
> —*With Open Hands*

Compassionate Care

What is compassion and its relationship to our call to mission? Compassion literally means "to suffer with." Compassion has to do with "taking part in the suffering of the other, being totally a fellow-human-being in suffering" (*LM*:31). Thus, to Nouwen, "a compassionate life is a life in which the suffering of others is deeply felt" (*IM*:29). We feel true compassion as soon as we connect with another person's experience of pain and suffering.

Nouwen assigns the same basic meaning to care as he does to compassion: "Care is being with, crying out with, suffering with, feeling with" (*BJ*:Feb 8). Real care is not vague. Real care "excludes indifference and is the opposite of apathy" (*OS*:33). To express real compassionate caring, we must always incorporate "empathetic awareness of the inner suffering and unique blessedness of those to whom we offer care" (*SC*:40).

For Nouwen, it is not possible to separate the idea of care from the true practice of compassion. Authentic ministry involves the attitude of compassionate caring and the exercise of caring compassionately.

A Heart That Cares

A heart that cares is a giving heart. It holds the ability to go out of one's self for another's sake. "Caregiving," Nouwen maintains, "is a deeply ingrained human response to suffering" (*SC*:26). He strongly believes that compassionate caregiving is what makes us true human beings who bear God's own image. To elaborate:

> Caring is the privilege of every person and is at the heart of being human. When we look at the original meaning of the word *profession* and realize that the term refers, first of all, to professing one's own deepest conviction, then the essential spiritual unity between living and caring becomes clear. (*GG*:51–52)

Thus Nouwen can say, "In the realm of the Spirit of God, living and caring are one" (*GG*:51). And to live one's life involved in the care of others "is the most human of all human gestures" (*SC*:16).

At the same time, for us to effectively care for others, it is imperative that we care for ourselves to begin with. Self-care presupposes that we love ourselves enough so we can freely love others. For to care is to love, with genuine attention, someone who is as much a child of God as we are (*GG*:58). As Nouwen puts it, "Caring for others is, first of all, helping them to overcome that enormous temptation of self-rejection" (*GG*:60). Nouwen points out that "we will never be able to really care if we are not willing to paint and repaint constantly our self-portrait, not as a morbid self-preoccupation, but as a service to those who are searching for some light in the midst of the darkness" (*AG*:95).

Henri Nouwen highlights two main characteristics of a caring person: poverty and compassion. Poverty refers to the quality of a caring heart willing to rid itself of any illusion of ownership and create room for others who are looking for a restful place. As Nouwen states, "When our hands, heads, and hearts are filled with worries, concerns, and preoccupations, there can hardly be any place left for the stranger to feel at home" (*AG*:106).

"To care is to be human."

—*Bread for the Journey*

Compassion, in this specific context, is about our capacity to feel and identify with those who are suffering while offering a hopeful place where weakness can be converted into strength. These two—poverty and compassion— are "the essentials of our self-portrait," according to Nouwen, "which we have to keep painting if we expect to be healers to those we encounter in the midst of despair and confusion" (*AG*:114–115).

Caring and Healing Beyond Cure

Caring means "first of all to be present to each other" in a manner that conveys a healing presence (*OS*:36). A heart that truly cares is willing to "offer one's own vulnerable self to others as a source of healing" (*AG*:97). This is what it means to participate in another's pain, to be in solidarity in suffering as well as to share in the other's experience of brokenness. However, caring is not to be equated with *cure*. In fact, "one of the great riches of caregiving is that it embraces something more than simply a focus on cure" (*SC*:16).

Care, for Nouwen, is uppermost, far above cure. For "cure without care is as dehumanizing as a gift given with a cold heart" (*OS*:32). We can always express care, but cure is not something we can guarantee to anyone. But each time we claim our gift of care, "we can become a true source of healing and hope. When we have the courage to let go of our need to cure, our care can truly heal in ways far beyond our own dreams and expectations" (*GG*:104). There is so much potency in our every attempt to care for others when our inner disposition is in the right place: seeking to bring about healing more than anything.

Mutual and Communal Caregiving

The basis of community life revolves around our capacity to care together. Henri Nouwen clarifies the mutual and communal facets: "Together we reach out to others. Together we look at those who need our care. Together we carry our suffering brothers and sisters to the place of rest, healing, and safety" (*GG*:64). At the heart of every community is our pledge of commitment to each other that is primarily driven out of love (*GG*:64).

Caring is not just a way to the self but, even more importantly, a way to the other; that is "the core of all caring: to be always present to each other. Caring is the way to the other by which a healing community becomes possible" (*AG*:120). The communal thrust of caregiving for Nouwen cannot be overemphasized. Lest we forget, "to care is to enter into the world of those who are broken and powerless and to establish there a fellowship of the weak. To care is to be present to those who suffer, and to stay present, even when

"Caring together is the basis of community life."

—*Our Greatest Gift*

nothing can be done to change their situation" (SC:16). The caring community in and of itself can indeed be an authentic healing community.

Henri Nouwen also brings our attention to the mutual benefits we derive from the ministry of caregiving, for it "carries within it an opportunity for inner healing, liberation, and transformation for the one being cared for and for the one who cares" (SC:16–17). This very aspect of mutuality enhances the sense of communal experience and contributes immensely to the building up of the community as a whole. Nouwen states even more specifically our communal gain by pointing out the great mystery of care: "When the one who is cared for and the one who cares come together in common vulnerability, then both experience a new community, both open themselves to conversion, and both experience new life as grace" (SC:54). Finally, "caregiving is ... receiving God's blessing from those to whom we give care. What is the blessing? It is a glimpse of the face of God" (SC:66). Nouwen is right: "One of the most beautiful characteristics of the compassionate life is that there is always a mutuality of giving and receiving" (HN:107).

Caring and Confronting

A compassionate, caring ministry can at the same time be a confrontational ministry. Henri Nouwen never views these characteristics as antithetical to each other. "Compassion without confrontation," he reasons, "fades quickly into fruitless commiseration" (C:124). Nouwen insists that in our ministry work we need to surround ourselves with both "encouragers" and "discouragers" and seek to be both to others as we carry out our call to compassionate living (RO:137). We certainly can use cheerleaders and supporters on our journey, particularly when

> "Confrontation ... is the radical side of care."
>
> —*Aging*

things get tough. But we can likewise profit from those who might discourage us from moving too rashly in life and might encourage us to rethink our way. We ourselves must strive to balance being loving affirmers on one hand and being bold truth-tellers on the other, who can point out others' as well as our own blind spots.

For Nouwen, genuine caring for others includes acceptance and confrontation. First, this "requires an ever-increasing acceptance," the kind that "led Jesus and his disciples to where they did not want to go—to the cross" (OH:60). By acceptance, Nouwen is referring not to some passive resignation or agreement with the facts of life, but to a bold posture of facing squarely or even confronting the stark reality of life. Quite the opposite though, "care is more than helping people to accept their fate. Real care includes confrontation" (AG:134). Confrontation can be construed as the total flip side of care:

> It promotes a risky detachment from the concerns of the world and a free manifestation of that love which can change the shape of our society. It not only unmasks the illusions but also makes visible the healing light that gives us the "power to become children of God [John 1:12]." (AG:141)

Nouwen is thus convinced that "ministry is a very confronting service" because it disallows people from living with certain illusions about wholeness (WH:93). Therefore it is the primary aim of everyone who truly cares "to prevent people ... from clinging to false expectations and from building their lives on false suppositions" (AG:137). Sometimes the most loving, caring thing to do for others is to expose the idols they are latching on to to make life work for them.

Lest we overlook an important dimension of confrontation, Nouwen directs our attention to the reality of the two fronts we have to deal with: inner and outer. For confrontation to retain its compassionate scope, the inner and the outer must always go hand in hand. Our own human heart is always in the equation, and Nouwen points to our constant need for self-confrontation. It is a gift, he says, that we find not easy to receive but nonetheless "a gift that can teach us much and help us in our own search for wholeness and holiness" (HN:109).

For Further Focused Reading

Aging: The Fulfillment of Life

Our Greatest Gift: A Meditation on Dying and Caring

A Spirituality of Caregiving

Living It Out

1. Ask God to bring to your heart a person in dire need or currently in the thick of suffering. Pray for a tangible way to express loving care for that person, by either calling or visiting him and allowing yourself to be a healing presence to and for him. Do for the other person whatever feels right for you and flows out of who you genuinely are inside. You may wish to journal about this experience and pray through it.

2. Nouwen emphasizes that we can only give away what we possess. Do a brief self-assessment and inventory of what you do deliberately for your own self-care as well as for exercising self-compassion. If nothing intentional is presently in place for you, think about some of the things you can do to address this.

3. Is there a loved one you genuinely care about who you know needs loving confrontation about something? Pray for this individual right now. Prayerfully discern how you might minister to her by being a caring truth-teller who is unafraid to risk confrontation as called for. Be sure you are motivated out of a deep compassionate care for the other person.

Prayer of the Heart

God who cares,

You have created, redeemed, and sustained us—not only because you love each of us, but because you genuinely, passionately care about every one of your children. You have seen and heard me, you have emptied yourself on my behalf and suffered for and with me, offering me the rest and hope that I have needed so desperately, making me dissatisfied with anything but your love. And now that I find myself in you, I find that same love increasing within me. Walk gently with me into my own suffering, and then help me to be less fearful of the suffering of those around me, so that my wounds in yours can bring your caring touch to this world.

Amen.

NINE

Hospitality

A Spacious Heart

"Hospitality ... means primarily the creation
of a free space where the stranger can enter
and become a friend instead of an enemy.
Hospitality is not to change people, but to
offer them space where change can take place."
—*Reaching Out*

For Henri Nouwen, ministry is all about practicing hospitality, and hospitality represents the true essence of an authentic ministry. His balanced take on hospitality is perhaps the most expansive and most nuanced treatment of hospitality as a spiritual practice of ministry. As Nouwen defines it in its most basic sense, hospitality centers on the creation of space—open, free, empty, friendly, empowering—for others. This is in stark contrast to what Nouwen refers to as occupied and preoccupied spaces, with which we are only too familiar. Just how does Nouwen understand space?

Henri Nouwen's concept of creating space is relationally oriented—according others high regard, offering them unconditional respect, and bestowing honor. Thus, for Nouwen, the task of creating space means a lot more than giving people margins or allowances as a gesture of tolerance. Rather, it is about empowering others as the God-imaged people

93

that they genuinely are—well-deserving of the highest value and respect. Little wonder that Nouwen admits to the reality that "creating space for the other is far from an easy task. It requires hard concentration and articulate work" (RO:72).

Creating Inner and Outer Space

It stands to reason that before we can offer others space, we ourselves must enjoy having such space. Consistent with the language of hospitality, Nouwen speaks of interior space in terms of "being at home in our own house" (RO:101). He talks about his own vivid realization of its importance: "I must create some free space in my innermost self so that I may indeed invite others to enter and be healed" (GD:145). He emphasizes the truth that "no guest will ever feel welcome when his host is not at home in his own house" (AG:102). For Nouwen, home is where we feel truly safe; when we come home and stay at home, we discover there the love that puts our hearts to rest (IVL:12). For Nouwen, at-homeness is possible only through engagement in solitude.

In order to create interior space for ourselves—and be able to offer others space—our own persistent loneliness must be converted into solitude. Nouwen is skeptical about our capacity to exercise hospitality as long as we are wrapped up in our lonely state, because "our own need to still our inner cravings of loneliness makes us cling to others instead of creating space for them" (RO:101). No healthy relationship can develop when we reach out to others from our loneliness; it can only have suffocating and destructive effects in the long run (BJ:Jan 19). Henri Nouwen himself succumbed to this very temptation that he warned others to avoid—entering "an intimacy and closeness that does not leave any open space," since "much suffering results from this suffocating closeness" (CR:40). And Nouwen did suffer much—and so did his relationship with Nathan Ball when Ball decided to distance himself from Nouwen out of a feeling of suffocation from Nouwen's incessant and impossible demands on him. Through this harrowing experience, Nouwen learned his lesson well, and fortunately their interrupted friendship was eventually restored.

In retrospect, Henri Nouwen concludes that the way to overcome our own dispiriting emotions, including a deep sense of aloneness and loneliness, is by "building a deeper sense of safety and at-homeness and a more incarnate knowledge that [we] are deeply loved" (*IVL*:42–43). Our inner spiritual home is the place we can return to each time we are plagued by doubt, for it is there that we can keep listening to the inner voice of love again and again (*IVL*:93).

Hospitable Space: Friendly, Empty, Open, and Free

A truly hospitable host, according to Nouwen, is one whose space is widely open and free—emptied of all sorts of occupations and preoccupations. Quite to the contrary, most of us live a cluttered, overbusy, and overextended life. We do not have any space left to give to others or to receive from them. Often we find ourselves only too eager to fill up our lives with every conceivable thing, including junk. Engaging in hospitality, says Nouwen, involves risk taking because "when we create an empty space, we make room for something to happen to us that we cannot predict, something that might really be new and lead us to places we would rather not go" (*SL*:15). Hospitality is freeing and even empowering and involves opening up "a wide spectrum of options for choice and commitment" (*RO*:71–72).

> "Hospitality is not a subtle invitation to adopt the lifestyle of the host, but the gift of a chance for the guest to find his own."
>
> —*Reaching Out*

Henri Nouwen illuminates the paradoxical nature of exercising hospitality:

> The paradox of hospitality is that it wants to create emptiness, not a fearful emptiness, but a friendly emptiness where strangers can enter and discover themselves as created free; free to sing their own songs, speak their own languages, dance their own dances; free to also leave and follow their own vocations. (*RO*:72)

Indeed, there is something inviting about a friendly, empty, open, and free space that makes people feel unintimidated and unthreatened. The reality is that we cannot pressure others to change through persuasion or unsolicited suggestions and advice. However, we can certainly provide them space where they are motivated "to disarm themselves, to lay aside their occupations and preoccupations and to listen with attention and care to the voices speaking in their own center" (*RO*:76). People naturally close off when they sense any attempt at manipulation from others. Conversely, they open up more when given plenty of breathing room to be themselves without any tinge of pressure. Ultimately, the generous extension of spaciousness spells all the difference.

Concentrated Focus and Communal Focus

Focused hospitality has two vital thrusts: concentration and community. First of all, "hospitality is the ability to pay attention to the guest" (*WH*:89). It is all too easy to be distracted by our preoccupations with our own insights, perspectives, and opinions so "that we have no space left to listen to the other and learn from him or her" (*OS*:42). Listening itself, Nouwen points out, is a generous form of hospitality, since it involves "paying full attention to others and welcoming them into our very beings" (*BJ*:Mar 11).

More often than not, we find it hard to pay attention because of our agenda-driven intentions. Here again Nouwen stresses the fact that "anyone who wants to pay attention without intention has to be at home in his own house—that is, he has to discover the center of his life in his own heart." Concentration, reinforced by the practice of meditation and contemplation, "is therefore the necessary precondition for true hospitality" (*WH*:90).

> "Anyone who wants to pay attention ... has to discover the center of his life in his own heart."
>
> —*The Wounded Healer*

By humbly withdrawing into ourselves, we can actually create space for others to be themselves and to come to us on their own terms without feeling pressure to conform to what we want (*WH*:91). Nouwen explains how our secure sense of groundedness can prove to be freeing for others:

When we are not afraid to enter into our own center and to concentrate on the stirrings of our own soul, we come to know that ... we can only give because life is a gift, and that we can only make others free because we are set free by him whose heart is greater than ours. When we have found the anchor places for our lives in our own center, we can be free to let others enter into the space created for them and allow them to dance their own dance, sing their own song and speak their own language without fear. Then our presence is no longer threatening and demanding but inviting and liberating. (WH:91–92)

Concentrated focus as an essential element of hospitality is very much related to the concept of exercising poverty of mind and heart, which we touched on in chapter 3 (see RO:103ff.).

In terms of communal focus, we are perennially reminded—all of us, all the time, as a people living in solidarity—of the sobering condition of our mortality and brokenness. And in our common search for life and healing, "hospitality becomes community" even "as it creates a unity based on the shared confession of our basic brokenness and on a shared hope" (WH:93). Not only is hospitality transformed into community, but more particularly, it becomes a healing community where "wounds and pains become openings or occasions for a new vision" (WH:94).

> "It is indeed the paradox of hospitality that poverty makes a good host."
>
> —*Reaching Out*

Moreover, "mutual confession then becomes a mutual deepening of hope, and sharing weakness becomes a reminder to one and all of the coming strength" (WH:94).

Creating Space Through Absence

To tackle the ministry and service of hospitality without dealing with the whole dynamic of presence is almost inconceivable. Hospitality and presence naturally go hand in hand. But beyond the powerful construct of presence, which Nouwen himself fully embodied in his ministry of companioning people, he introduces us all to a seemingly antithetical way of creating space for others—and that is through what he calls the ministry of absence.

Just as hospitality naturally requires what Nouwen refers to as "articulate presence," it likewise demands the employment of its counterpart: creative absence. Nouwen is persuaded that there are times when "we have to learn to leave so that the Spirit can come" (LR:45). For it is true that there are occasions on which we find ourselves more of a hindrance than a help to others by standing in the way of what God is doing; we occupy space that is better assigned to the Holy Spirit. Sometimes we need to be willing to abandon our claim to space and give way to the Spirit to freely work in other people without our help or presence. Because we often insist on nourishing our illusion of indispensability, we need to be reminded that God continues to be actively at work in people's lives even without us. Instead of potentially being in the way, we can more intentionally point others to the Way. Indeed "there is a ministry in which our leaving creates space for God's Spirit and in which, by our absence, God can become present in a new way" (LR:44).

There is a sense in which generous and spacious hospitality asks us to create dual space: a space for others, breathing room without our sometimes stifling presence and overavailability; and a space for God, the Spirit, to allow for God's unhindered way to work in people's lives in any way God chooses. For instance, in a ministry of visitation—whether it be hospital or home visits—"it is essential for patients and parishioners to experience that it is good for them, not only that we come but also that we leave" (LR:44). Unfortunately, there are times when we lack the sensitivity to discern the appropriate timing of when to come and when to go. Our withdrawal must be purposeful. Nouwen suggests using "a plea for prayer as the creative way of being unavailable" (LR:49). Though we may be physically absent from people, there is a sense in which we are present with them in spirit even as we pray for them in our absence. As he concludes, "When our absence from people means a special presence to God, then that absence becomes a sustaining absence" (LR:50).

> "There is a ministry in which our leaving creates space for God's Spirit."
> —The Living Reminder

This tensional interplay between presence and absence holds true in our exercise of hospitality toward both those outside our communities and those within them. Our way of being present to our community may indeed require spacious times of absence. Nouwen puts it this way:

> Your community needs you, but maybe not as a constant presence. Your community might need you as a presence that offers courage and spiritual food for the journey, a presence that creates the safe ground in which others can grow and develop, a presence that belongs to the matrix of the community. But your community also needs your creative absence. (IVL:68)

Knowing when to be present or absent can understandably be a challenge. Still, we need to learn how to creatively navigate our way through this tension so we can best cooperate with God. To be a hospitable soul host with, to, and for others calls for a spacious heart—a heart able to create and offer both interior space for one's self and exterior space for others, as well as a discerning heart that wisely knows how to exercise "creative absence."

For Further Focused Reading

The Inner Voice of Love: A Journey Through Anguish to Freedom
Reaching Out: The Three Movements of the Spiritual Life
The Wounded Healer

Living It Out

1. Put into practice the idea of "being at home in your own house" through some form of mindfulness (or heartfulness) meditation exercise. Embrace the "sacrament of the present moment" by creating space to be completely still—at home with yourself and who you are in God—for a good twenty minutes. Alternatively, try doing a mental body scan—from head to toe and back to head—just listening to your body and your sensations nonjudgmentally. Gently connect with and embrace your body.

2. Cultivate hospitality to someone by exercising poverty of mind and heart (see chapter 3). Offer generous space to a friend by just being with her, listening, and welcoming whatever your friend wishes to share, consciously refraining from saying anything; let your communication be simply a gesture of silent affirmation or validation.

3. Pray for an opportunity this week to extend hospitality to a complete stranger without any compelling agenda to change or fix the other person. Choose to empower the stranger to be who he is by celebrating his uniqueness in whatever way you discern to be appropriate.

Prayer of the Heart

God who welcomes me,

Show me today when I am open to you and to those around me, as well as when I am closed to you and those you have put into my life. I want deeply to have more open space for you in my life, and for it to be a space that offers peace to others. Yet so many things in my life fill up the space and prevent me from being with you and from genuinely being with others. Most of them are good things, yet still they create clutter in who I am. I need your wisdom today, Lord, to know which things to clear out and which things are genuinely mine to be used for your glory. If something needs to go so that I can have more open space to offer, help me to loosen my grip on it, and if something should stay, may it be used freely as your gift for the sake of others.

In the name of the One who is preparing a place for me.

Amen.

CONCLUSION

Mere Spirituality

It has been almost half a century since Henri Nouwen published *Intimacy*, his first work on the spiritual life. Even then, he already evidenced the voice of a prophet whose pulse on the climate of the Church is as accurate today as it was at that time. Not much has changed; Nouwen's analysis of the spiritual landscape still rings very true:

> The churches, in many ways entangled in their own structural problems, often seem hardly ready to respond to this growing need to live a spiritual life. The tragedy is that many find the church more in the way to God than the way to God, and are looking for religious experiences far away from the ecclesiastical institutions. But if we read the signs well we are on the threshold of a new era of spiritual life, the nature and ramifications of which we can hardly foresee. Hopefully, we will not be distracted by the trivia of churchy family quarrels and overlook the great questions which really matter. Hopefully, we will be sensitive enough to feel the gentle breeze by which God makes his presence known. (*I*:150)

God truly is in the business of always making all things new. The promise of the spiritual life remains ours to claim at any given time if we care to do so. The basic question is, what kind of spiritual life are we to embrace?

By now it is clear that by "spiritual life" Nouwen is pointing to our life in the Spirit—one that has to do with "the nurturing of the eternal amid the temporal, the lasting within the passing, God's presence in the human family. It is the life of the divine Spirit within us" (*TMD*:48). As simple as that may appear, Nouwen has no qualms about admitting that living a spiritual life is never easy (*SD*:17). At the same time, he is quite certain that "living a spiritual life is living a life in which the Holy Spirit will guide us and give us the strength and courage to keep saying *yes* to the great question—Can you drink the cup?" (*CDC*:107).

From his own life experience, Nouwen could verify with clearheadedness the reality that "the whole course of the spiritual life is falling off, and returning, slipping away from the truth and turning back to it, leaving and returning" (*HT*:41). None of us can claim to have fully arrived; we are always in the process of arriving. Here Nouwen issues a word of caution: "Those who think that they have arrived have lost their way. Those who think they have reached their goal have missed it" (*GD*:133). Likewise, he directs our consciousness to the truth that "an important part of the spiritual life is to keep longing, waiting, hoping, expecting" (*GD*:133). The reassuring reality is that "our spiritual life is a life in which we wait, actively present to the moment, expecting that new things will happen to us, new things that are far beyond our own imagination or prediction. This, indeed, is a very radical stance toward life in a world preoccupied with control" (*FWH*:103).

Nouwen notes the inclination of many of us to construe the spiritual life as occurring only when "we have certain feelings, think certain thoughts, or gain certain insights"—realities that are not within our power to effect. Our task, he points out, "is not how to make the spiritual life happen, but to see where it actually is happening" and to simply detect that, in fact, "it is God who is acting, and we are involved already in the spiritual life" (*SD*:20). God is constantly at work.

"The mystery of the spiritual life," says Nouwen, "is that many of the events, people, and situations that for a long time seemed to inhibit our way to God become ways of our being united more deeply with him. What seemed a hindrance proves to be a gift" (*CFM*:123). Everything sovereignly and providentially revolves around our ultimate union with God. Communion is the beginning and the end of our spiritual life, for "in and through the Spirit we become full participants in the communion of love that Jesus shares with his Father. That is the mystery of our redemption and the promise of the spiritual life" (*SL*:22). What a high privilege it is for us to embark on a spiritual journey "in which we are lifted up to become partakers of the divine life" (*MTN*:54).

The Spiritual Life According to Henri Nouwen

So what does our spiritual life encompass? Nouwen presents three distinct but interrelated characteristics. First, it is a life *apart*, a life consecrated to God involving a certain "withdrawal" from the world to be in communion with God in solitude. But this withdrawal is always a temporary one because reengagement is necessary for the survival and sustenance of our spiritual life. Therefore, it is equally a life *shared* in and with a community of like-minded people who are at the same time diverse in many different ways. Lastly, it is a life *given* by means of service as a ministry toward others in the world.

The spiritual life according to Nouwen consists of engaging in an ongoing *communion* with God, deepening our experience of *community* with each other, and responding to God's *commission* to serve and minister to a world in need. Communion, community, and commission are not to be viewed as independent realities but rather as interdependent ones. They work together to fuel the engine of our spiritual life.

A Life Apart

What does it mean to have a spiritual life except to live life "in an intimate communion with the Lord" (*SWC*:15)? Doing so involves making a priority of extravagantly wasting time with and for God. How do we do this while immersed in our daily existence? To start with, we need to recognize that our spiritual life "is contained in the most simple, ordinary experiences of everyday living" (*GD*:41). Additionally, Nouwen reminds us that "the spiritual life is not a life before, after, or beyond our everyday existence.... The spiritual life can only be real when it is lived in the midst of the pains and joys of the here and now" (*MTN*:21).

Henri Nouwen articulates for us the essence of the spiritual life: "to live in the world without belonging to the world" (*BBL*:19). Existentially, it means living in but apart from the world. To do this requires, first and foremost, the cultivation of a heart that is deeply intimate with God and one's self through a consistent discipline of solitude. Second, it demands a well-grounded, centered heart whose identity is securely fastened on one's belovedness before God. Finally, it means having a heart attentive to the threefold sacrament of presence: presence to self, to others, and to the very sacred Presence itself.

A Life Shared

The spiritual life thrives in a balanced rhythm of withdrawal and reengagement. We need to disappear every so often and go to hidden places so we can reappear with renewed spiritual vigor. We need to learn to be alone so we can savor the fellowship of a community, in the same way that we need the support of the community in order to enjoy being alone with and for God.

Nouwen does not mind repeating again and again the fact that "a life in the Spirit is in essence a life in community," because there is no way we can separate "belonging to God from belonging to each other and seeing Christ from seeing one another in him" (*BBL*:59–60). To this, he adds, "Seeing Christ leads us to the heart of God as well as to the heart of all that is human. It is a sacred event in which contemplation and compassion are one, and in which we are prepared for an eternal life of seeing" (*BBL*:56).

God's call, more than anything, is what makes a sense of togetherness as a community a living reality. Love and unity are the spiritual glue that bonds our hearts in one accord. Our commonality of heart—our universal calling, our humanity, our vulnerability—is what highlights our mutuality and the reality that we need to complement each other in our strengths and weaknesses as a community. Finally, we are in solidarity because we belong to each other with hearts connected tightly by our sameness more than our so-called differences. Our togetherness, mutuality, and solidarity are such an intertwining communal affair that it is virtually impossible to segregate one from the other. All combined, they reflect the gift of community for nurturing our spiritual life.

A Life Given

The communal life we enjoy is not just for our own benefit. In Nouwen's words, expressed as a prayer to Jesus, "It is also a life that calls me to give all that I am in the service of your love for the world" (*HSH*:43). As he declares emphatically, the inner life we share together "is always a life for others" (*GG*:6). Nouwen consistently stresses the outward thrust of community. As a community, we are called to minister together to the larger community of the world. This is our commission—to willingly give our lives away in the service of others. Nouwen himself testifies, "As the Beloved ones, our greatest fulfillment lies in becoming bread for the world. That is the most intimate expression of our deepest desire to give ourselves to each other"— both in life and in death (*LB*:89). In many ways, every form of ministry is about life-giving—that is, giving our lives to others. At the same time, ministry in and of itself is a life-giving venture: we give our lives in order to give life—new life—to ourselves as well as others.

The nature of our common mission is first to serve and give of ourselves selflessly and sacrificially for others' sake as modeled to us by our Lord, the suffering servant. Laying down our lives for others assumes that we do in fact have a full self to give and a life to lay down, for we cannot give out something we do not possess. This brings us back to the cycle of communion, where we nurture this life of ours in God so we can minister out of the abundance of God's life flowing through us. Second, our mission requires a caring heart, willing and able to identify and connect with the suffering of others on an experiential level. It is a heart that cares enough not simply to accept others but also to confront them when that is called for. It is a heart that beats with the compassion of Jesus for others. Third, our call is characterized by a quality of hospitality made possible by a spacious heart generous enough to offer people a free, empty, friendly, and open space to allow change in them to take its own natural course. For Henri Nouwen, all ministry is about hospitality, and hospitality is what genuine ministry truly is. A life given in and for ministry is a life responsive to God's commission to engage in selfless service, caring compassion, and spacious hospitality.

Henri Nouwen spoke about the spiritual life every time he had the chance. Most importantly, he lived it out to the best of his ability. His life was a shining example of a life apart, a life shared, and a life given. On his journey, he embodied the experiential realities of communion, community, and commission with passionate devotion. He did not allow himself to be distracted from what he felt was his overarching vocation: to teach and live the true nature of our spiritual life in God. Everything he was about emanated from the spirituality he believed in, lived out, and espoused to one and all—mere spirituality.

Acknowledgments

The concept behind this book has been on my mind for about four years. I thank Emily Wichland of SkyLight Paths Publishing, who showed genuine interest in this endeavor the very first time I shared about its prospect. She followed it through all the way. As well, I am indebted to Rachel Shields for her remarkable editorial skills and keen attention to detail. The end result of her conscientious work is a much more polished product with which I am well pleased.

As with my three previous works on Nouwen, I wrote large portions of the manuscript in various retreat centers where I either presented a retreat or attended one. But the bulk of the writing took place at my favorite monastery, where I serve as a lay Benedictine oblate—Saint Andrew's Abbey in Valyermo, California. I am grateful to Father Patrick for accommodating me each time there was a vacancy in Kirby Room. The monastic setting and rhythm proved to be ideal for the disciplined focus I needed to complete this ambitious project.

I am more than delighted that Father Ron Rolheiser, OMI, has written the foreword for this book—all for the love of Nouwen. He took the time to call me personally just to let me know how honored he was to do it, even before he had a chance to read the entire manuscript. I would jump at the opportunity to teach the contents of this work at the Oblate School of Theology, where he serves as president. (I taught a two-week Nouwen course there several years ago, and I would not mind going back again!) Father Ron, please consider this an official invitation—my bold way of inviting myself in exchange for your generous heart!

Gratitude also goes to Paul Johansen, whose little essay on Nouwen containing the phrase "mere spirituality" triggered in me the idea—and the very title—for this book. It is not my intention to be pretentious, ambitious, or even presumptuous, due to the title's association with C. S. Lewis's classic work *Mere Christianity*. I chose the title because Henri Nouwen, by any measure, truly embodies the phrase.

Daniel Ethan Harris, one of my former spiritual directees and a participant in our inaugural cohort of the CenterQuest School of Spiritual Direction, crafted a unique "prayer of the heart" at the end of each chapter in the book. Thanks, Daniel, for being able to capture the heart of Henri Nouwen through these moving prayers on the theme of each chapter.

Finally, I want to thank our CenterQuest Community of Companions for their prayers and support as I embarked on this writing project amid all the hectic preparations involved in the launch of the inaugural cohort for our School of Spiritual Direction. I would not have made it to the finish line without you being there for me in countless ways.

God's grace allowed me to witness two "births" this year: the birth of CenterQuest's School of Spiritual Direction and the birth of this book on Nouwen—both of which emerged out of the many huge, almost insurmountable challenges that came with the territory of creating something new. Both experiences forced me, in a good way, to always go to the center, the hub, and there embrace the centerpoint, which is also the stillpoint that makes all things possible ... and new. Thanks be to God!

A Chronology of Henri Nouwen's Life and Works

The Formative Years in Holland: 1932–1964

1932   Born January 24 to Maria and Laurent Nouwen in Nijkerk, the Netherlands.

1950–1957   Entered the Minor Seminary in Apeldoorn in 1950; moved to the Major Seminary in Rijsenburg a year after and stayed until his priestly ordination in the Diocese of Utrecht on July 21, 1957.

1957–1964   Started graduate studies in psychology at the Catholic University of Nijmegen and finished course work on February 3, 1964.

1961–1963   Served as an army chaplain for the Dutch army.

The Menninger Clinic Years: 1964–1966

Moved to the United States and became a fellow at the Menninger Clinic in Topeka, Kansas, under its religion and psychiatry program. While there, he finished his clinical pastoral education (CPE) training at Topeka State Hospital.

Adapted from the biographical time line of Henri's life posted at the Henri J. M. Nouwen Archives and Research Collection website (http://usmccollections.library. utoronto.ca/content/biographical-timeline) and the chronological bibliography of Nouwen's books posted at the Henri Nouwen Society website (www.henrinouwen. org/books/bibliography/chronological/chronological%20order.aspx).

The Notre Dame Years: 1966–1968

Joined the faculty of the newly formed department of psychology at the University of Notre Dame in Indiana as a visiting professor, teaching courses in clinical and pastoral psychology, among several others. While there, he started working on his first book, *Intimacy*, culled from several of his course lectures and sermons and published a year after his leaving the university in 1968.

Back to the Netherlands: 1968–1971

Upon his return to Holland, he accepted positions to teach at the Amsterdam Joint Pastoral Institute and then at the Catholic Theological Institute of Utrecht, where he headed the department of behavioral sciences.

Pursued advanced theological studies at the University of Nijmegen, focusing on the work of Anton Boisen, the founder of clinical pastoral education, and received a doctorandus degree in 1971.

- *Intimacy* (1969)
- *Creative Ministry* (1971)

The Yale Years: 1971–1981

1971 Moved back to the United States after accepting a position to teach pastoral theology at Yale Divinity School.

1972 Published *The Wounded Healer*, a memorable title that has become the cornerstone of Nouwen's spirituality.

1974 Granted tenure at Yale.

Stayed as a temporary Trappist monk at the Abbey of the Genesee in upstate New York from June to December.

1976 Became a fellow at the Ecumenical Institute in Saint John's Abbey in Collegeville, Minnesota.

1977 Became full professor of pastoral theology at Yale.

1978 Mother became sick while visiting at Yale in September and died of an inoperable cancer on October 9 upon returning to Holland.

1979 Returned to the Abbey of the Genesee from February to August.

1981 Gave up tenure at Yale and resigned from his teaching position in July at forty-nine years old.

- *Thomas Merton: Contemplative Critic* (1972)
- *With Open Hands* (1972)
- *The Wounded Healer* (1972)
- *Out of Solitude* (1974)
- *Aging* (1974)
- *Reaching Out* (1975)
- *The Genesee Diary* (1976)
- *The Living Reminder* (1977)
- *Clowning in Rome* (1979)
- *In Memoriam* (1980)
- *Making All Things New* (1981)

Latin America/Harvard/L'Arche Interlude: 1981–1985

1981–1982 Studied Spanish for three months in Bolivia and spent another three months living with a family in a poor barrio in Lima, Peru, while engaging in mission work with the poor under the guidance of the Maryknoll community.

1982 Returned to the United States in March. On August 6, 1982, celebrated the twenty-fifth anniversary of his priestly ordination at the Abbey of the Genesee.

1983 Accepted a part-time position to teach at Harvard. Spent a month in Mexico during the second half of 1983; traveled to Nicaragua and Honduras and afterward went on a whirlwind speaking tour in the United States, drawing attention to the oppression occurring in Central America.

Visited L'Arche in Trosly, France, for the first time in the fall of 1983.

1984 Traveled to Guatemala from August 27 to September 5 at the invitation of Father John Vesey, who had taken over the job of martyred priest Stanley Rother. Nouwen wrote about Rother's moving story in a book called *Love in a Fearful Land*, published a year later.

Traveled back to Trosly in December for a thirty-day retreat.

1985 Left Harvard at the end of his third trimester there.

1985–1986 Spent a year at L'Arche in Trosly, from August 1985 to August 1986.

Made a ten-day visit to L'Arche Daybreak in Toronto, October 1–10. Received a formal invitation from L'Arche Daybreak community on December 12 to be their resident pastor.

- *The Way of the Heart* (1981)
- *A Cry for Mercy* (1981)
- *Compassion* (1982)
- *A Letter of Consolation* (1982)
- *¡Gracias!* (1983)
- *Love in a Fearful Land* (1985)

The L'Arche Daybreak Years: 1986–1996

1986 Moved to Toronto at the end of August to become the pastor of the Daybreak community. Nouwen was assigned to be the direct-care assistant to Adam Arnett, one of the most severely disabled members at L'Arche.

1987 Returned to Cambridge, Massachusetts, to give a moving lecture on Adam to some five hundred people at Saint Paul Catholic Church.

1988 Suffered a nervous breakdown as a result of a relationship break with Nathan Ball. Entered into a treatment facility in Winnipeg for seven months.

1989 Involved in a van accident that nearly killed him.

1991 Met the South African trapeze artists known as the Flying Rodleighs, with whom he developed a close relationship over the years.

1992 Gave a series of homilies for Crystal Cathedral's televised *Hour of Power.* Published what would become one of his most, if not his most popular book, *The Return of the Prodigal Son,* based on his visit to the Hermitage in 1986 to see Rembrandt's original painting of the same name.

1995 Sent off by L'Arche Daybreak community for his sabbatical year beginning on September 2.

1996 Suffered a heart attack on September 15 while en route to Saint Petersburg to do a documentary film for his book *The Return of the Prodigal Son*. Died of a massive cardiac arrest on September 21 in Holland and was buried in the Sacred Heart Cemetery near Toronto, Canada, on September 28.

- *Lifesigns* (1986)
- *Behold the Beauty of the Lord* (1987)
- *The Road to Daybreak* (1988)
- *Letters to Marc about Jesus* (1988)
- *In the Name of Jesus* (1989)
- *Heart Speaks to Heart* (1989)
- *Walk with Jesus* (1990)
- *Beyond the Mirror* (1990)
- *Life of the Beloved* (1992)
- *The Return of the Prodigal Son* (1992)
- *Jesus and Mary* (1993)
- *Here and Now* (1994)
- *Our Greatest Gift* (1994)
- *With Burning Hearts* (1994)
- *The Path Series* (1995)
- *Ministry and Spirituality* (1996)
- *The Inner Voice of Love* (1996)
- *Can You Drink the Cup?* (1996)
- *Sabbatical Journey* (1997)
- *Adam* (1997)
- *Bread for the Journey* (1997)
- *Spiritual Journals* (1997)

Posthumous Publications: 1998–2013

- *The Road to Peace* (1998)
- *Finding My Way Home* (2001)
- *Turn My Mourning into Dancing* (2001)
- *Encounters with Merton* (2004)
- *A Spirituality of Fundraising* (2004)
- *Peacework* (2005)
- *Spiritual Direction* (2006)
- *The Selfless Way of Christ* (2007)

- *Home Tonight* (2009)
- *Spiritual Formation* (2010)
- *A Sorrow Shared* (2010)
- *Finding Our Sacred Center* (2011)
- *A Spirituality of Caregiving* (2011)
- *A Spirituality of Living* (2011)
- *Discernment* (2013)

Source Abbreviations

A	*Adam: God's Beloved*
AG	*Aging: The Fulfillment of Life*
B	*Beloved*
BBL	*Behold the Beauty of the Lord: Praying with Icons*
BH	*With Burning Hearts: A Meditation on the Eucharistic Life*
BJ	*Bread for the Journey: A Daybook of Wisdom and Faith*
BM	*Beyond the Mirror: Reflections on Death and Life*
C	*Compassion: A Reflection on the Christian Life*
CDC	*Can You Drink the Cup?*
CFM	*A Cry for Mercy: Prayers from the Genesee*
CM	*Creative Ministry*
CR	*Clowning in Rome: Reflections on Solitude, Celibacy, Prayer, and Contemplation*
D	*Discernment: Reading the Signs of Daily Life*
EM	*Encounters with Merton: Spiritual Reflections*
FSC	*Finding Our Sacred Center: A Journey to Inner Peace*
FWH	*Finding My Way Home: Pathways to Life and the Spirit*
G!	*¡Gracias! A Latin American Journal*
GD	*The Genesee Diary: Report from a Trappist Monastery*
GG	*Our Greatest Gift: A Meditation on Death and Dying*
HN	*Here and Now: Living in the Spirit*
HSH	*Heart Speaks to Heart: Three Prayers to Jesus*
HT	*Home Tonight: Further Reflections on the Parable of the Prodigal Son*
I	*Intimacy*

IM	*In Memoriam*
INJ	*In the Name of Jesus: Reflections on Christian Leadership*
IVL	*The Inner Voice of Love: A Journey Through Anguish to Freedom*
LB	*Life of the Beloved: Spiritual Living in a Secular World*
LC	*A Letter of Consolation*
LFL	*Love in a Fearful Land: A Guatemalan Story*
LM	*Letters to Marc about Jesus: Living a Spiritual Life in a Material World*
LR	*The Living Reminder: Service and Prayer in Memory of Jesus Christ*
LS	*Lifesigns: Intimacy, Fecundity, and Ecstasy in Christian Perspective*
MTN	*Making All Things New: An Invitation to the Spiritual Life*
OH	*With Open Hands: Bringing Prayer into Your Life*
OS	*Out of Solitude: Three Meditations on the Christian Life*
PW	*Peacework: Prayer, Resistance, Community*
RD	*The Road to Daybreak: A Spiritual Journey*
RO	*Reaching Out: The Three Movements of the Spiritual Life*
RP	*The Road to Peace*
RPS	*The Return of the Prodigal Son: A Story of Homecoming*
SC	*A Spirituality of Caregiving*
SD	*Spiritual Direction: Wisdom for the Long Walk of Faith*
SF	*Spiritual Formation: Following the Movements of the Spirit*
SJ	*Sabbatical Journey: The Diary of His Final Year*
SL	*A Spirituality of Living*
SWC	*The Selfless Way of Christ: Downward Mobility and the Spiritual Life*
TMD	*Turn My Mourning into Dancing: Finding Hope in Hard Times*
WH	*The Wounded Healer: Ministry in Contemporary Society*
WOH	*The Way of the Heart: Desert Spirituality and Contemporary Ministry*

Key Works of Henri Nouwen

Adam: God's Beloved. Maryknoll, NY: Orbis Books, 1997.

Aging: The Fulfillment of Life. With Walter J. Gaffney. New York: Image, 1990.

Behold the Beauty of the Lord: Praying with Icons. Notre Dame, IN: Ave Maria Press, 1987.

Beloved: Henri Nouwen in Conversation. With Philip Roderick. Ottawa: Novalis, 2007.

Beyond the Mirror: Reflections on Death and Life. New York: Crossroad, 2001.

Bread for the Journey: A Daybook of Wisdom and Faith. San Francisco: HarperSanFrancisco, 1982.

Can You Drink the Cup? Notre Dame, IN: Ave Maria Press, 1996.

Clowning in Rome: Reflections on Solitude, Celibacy, Prayer, and Contemplation. New York: Image, 2000.

Compassion: A Reflection on the Christian Life. New York: Image, 1983.

Creative Ministry. New York: Image, 1978.

A Cry for Mercy: Prayers from the Genesee. New York: Image, 1983.

Discernment: Reading the Signs of Daily Life. With Michael J. Christensen and Rebecca Laird. New York: HarperOne, 2013.

Encounters with Merton: Spiritual Reflections. New York: Crossroad, 1981.

Finding My Way Home: Pathways to Life and the Spirit. New York: Crossroad, 2001.

Finding Our Sacred Center: A Journey to Inner Peace. New London, CT: Twenty-Third Publications, 2011.

The Genesee Diary: Report from a Trappist Monastery. New York: Image, 1989.

¡Gracias! A Latin American Journal. Maryknoll, NY: Orbis Books, 1993.

Heart Speaks to Heart: Three Prayers to Jesus. Notre Dame, IN: Ave Maria Press, 1989.

Here and Now: Living in the Spirit. New York: Crossroad, 1994.

Home Tonight: Further Reflections on the Parable of the Prodigal Son. New York: Doubleday, 2009.

In Memoriam. Notre Dame, IN: Ave Maria Press, 1980.

The Inner Voice of Love: A Journey Through Anguish to Freedom. New York: Image, 1996.

In the Name of Jesus: Reflections on Christian Leadership. New York: Crossroad, 1989.

Intimacy. San Francisco: HarperSanFrancisco, 1969.

A Letter of Consolation. San Francisco: HarperSanFrancisco, 1982.

Letters to Marc about Jesus: Living a Spiritual Life in a Material World. San Francisco: HarperSanFrancisco, 1998.

Life of the Beloved: Spiritual Living in a Secular World. New York: Crossroad, 1992.

Lifesigns: Intimacy, Fecundity, and Ecstasy in Christian Perspective. New York: Doubleday, 1986.

The Living Reminder: Service and Prayer in Memory of Jesus Christ. San Francisco: HarperSanFrancisco, 1977.

Love in a Fearful Land: A Guatemalan Story. Maryknoll, NY: Orbis Books, 2006.

Making All Things New: An Invitation to the Spiritual Life. San Francisco: HarperSanFrancisco, 1981.

Our Greatest Gift: A Meditation on Death and Dying. New York: HarperCollins, 1995.

Out of Solitude: Three Meditations on the Christian Life. Notre Dame, IN: Ave Maria Press, 1974.

Peacework: Prayer, Resistance, Community. Maryknoll, NY: Orbis Books, 2006.

Reaching Out: The Three Movements of the Spiritual Life. New York: Doubleday, 1975.

The Return of the Prodigal Son: A Story of Homecoming. New York: Image, 1994.

The Road to Daybreak: A Spiritual Journey. New York: Doubleday, 1988.

The Road to Peace. Maryknoll, NY: Orbis Books, 1998.

Sabbatical Journey: The Diary of His Final Year. New York: Crossroad, 1998.

The Selfless Way of Christ: Downward Mobility and the Spiritual Life. Maryknoll, NY: Orbis Books, 2007.

Spiritual Direction: Wisdom for the Long Walk of Faith. New York: HarperOne, 2006.

Spiritual Formation: Following the Movements of the Spirit. New York: HarperOne, 2010.

A Spirituality of Caregiving. Nashville: Upper Room Books, 2011.

A Spirituality of Living. Nashville: Upper Room Books, 2011.

Turn My Mourning into Dancing: Finding Hope in Hard Times. Nashville: Word Publishing, 2001.

The Way of the Heart: Desert Spirituality and Contemporary Ministry. New York: HarperCollins, 1991.

The Wounded Healer: Ministry in Contemporary Society. New York: Image, 1979.

With Burning Hearts: A Meditation on the Eucharistic Life. Maryknoll, NY: Orbis Books, 1994.

With Open Hands: Bringing Prayer into Your Life. New York: Ballantine, 1985.

Credits

Source Index

An Ecumenical Hub
for the Study and Practice
of Christian Spirituality

For more information, check out
www.CQCenterQuest.org
or call 1-855-WHEEL-05.